THE
INNER
shift

The empowered path of shifting within to gain
purpose, prosperity, and peace

Seema Khan
HOLISTIC LIFE COACH

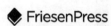 FriesenPress

One Printers Way
Altona, MB R0G 0B0
Canada

www.friesenpress.com

Book cover image design by: Ibraheem Rasheed
Interior mirror image design by: Ibraheem Rasheed
Leaf image design by: Seema Khan

ISBN
978-1-03-915235-9 (Hardcover)
978-1-03-915234-2 (Paperback)
978-1-03-915236-6 (eBook)

1. SELF-HELP, PERSONAL GROWTH, SELF-ESTEEM

Distributed to the trade by The Ingram Book Company

Dearest Sarah !
♡

May this work inspire
new deep conversations
within ♡

2024 .

Table of Contents

Introduction

I wrote this book to help the reader cultivate a passion for inner growth in attempts to lead a profoundly fulfilling and enriched life. My intention is to encourage you to explore and develop your own expansive inner state of being, which allows you to unleash your highest potential through reflective inner work, based on my practice as a life coach. I share concrete concepts, personal stories, guidelines, and simple reflective exercises to inspire you to become your best version, as I continuously remind myself through my own words. This book acts as an easily applicable guide for cultivating self-mastery.

What inspired me to write this book? Aside from the fact that expressive writing is cathartic and uplifting for my spirit, I highly value and aspire to live a wholesome and purposeful life. I truly believe that we can create the version of ourselves that can help us resolve our problems and allows us to prosper. I have also come to understand that such a goal is only achieved through deep inner work. And I want to play a role in helping people make their own *inner shifts* to get there.

I have been on my own journey of self-improvement for several years. When I personally overcame some of my own struggles, I went through a process of unlearning and relearning some life concepts which shifted my paradigm in a highly impactful way. I uncovered just how much power lies within me and was ready to claim it. I also realized that most people overlook the importance of intentional inner work. It certainly is a path less travelled! This work is for the daring few who challenge themselves to revisit old pattens, transform their mindsets, and break unhealthy cycles to uncover their best selves.

Somewhere on my path of personal discovery, I found my true calling. I became highly motivated to help others overcome their obstacles to live soulful lives full of exuberance, self-confidence, and peace, and free of bitterness, negativity, or victimhood.

Coaching women and witnessing massive life-altering results has been immensely fulfilling for my soul. However, I had this constant urge to amplify my impact and reach many more lives beyond one-on-one coaching. With my strong passion to help others, I decided to gather the essentials of my work and present it in the form of a self-help book, which is easy to understand and apply.

It has always been a dream for me to write a book. But there were hurdles. It seemed like a daunting impossible task which required commitment, learning, focus, consistency, and patience. Also, the fear of rejection and the heavy burden of responsibly wording things can cripple a creative process. I did hold back at first thinking, *Who am I to write a book?* We have been programmed to think that one must have to arrive at some high place of authority to be able to share a message and shine their light. Many don't even know what that position looks like or when one arrives there!

I believe that you can't relate any message that you don't embody yourself. Because then the message is vacant. So, I needed to make sure that I was at some level a living example of all that I passionately share in my writing. Writing a book comes with the uneasy feelings of self-promotion and placing oneself on a pedestal. You feel like you need to show yourself as an expert. I had to overcome such feelings to truly step into my element and write my heart out authentically and bravely share my message.

Soon enough, with all due humility, I realized that there is only one of me in this world, with my own distinctive thumb print. And perhaps what I can share through my unique words, will change someone's life. With that mindset and pure intention, I began to dream of a legacy to touch many lives through my words.

My mind began to burst with ideas, stories, and perspectives that I wanted to share. I became obsessed with studying relevant content from videos, articles, podcasts, books, and online sources. I learned different strategies and modalities under the influence of mentors, coaches, and therapists while drafting my own ideas based on reflections from my coaching sessions and some instant downloads from my introspective personal experiences. The more I learned, the more I wanted to share through my own lens. As my quest for becoming my own better version grew, so did the passion to inspire others alongside.

In the book in your hands, you'll find my humble attempt to present self-growth concepts illuminated by some quotes on various topics followed by detailed discussions including some vulnerable personal shares and simple reflections that you may connect with. A lot of the tools I share are really the core material from my coaching sessions with my clients, which will allow you to self-coach and reinvent yourself.

You can skim through the contents and choose the chapter that 'calls' to you as each chapter does not necessarily build on top of the other. However, some chapters may be related to other topics content-wise, but they are separate topics on their own as well. I recommend referring to related topics for clarity on concepts if needed. There is also space at the end of each chapter for doing some reflective work. I suggest pulling out your journal and reflect through writing.

Each chapter begins with an imperative topic, which calls you to personally connect and respond. I recommend reading each chapter slowly to allow the material to sink in so you can apply some of the concepts into your life and put some things into practice. It can be exciting to read inspirational content but 'walking the talk' is the real challenge. This is why life coaching exists, as we all need the necessary support and accountability to implement real life disciplines.

The initial chapters pertain to general self-discovery and development, building on to some paradigm-shifting inner work to breakthrough personal limitations, while the topics intensify towards the last third and become deeper and more spiritual. The intention is to ultimately attain a holistically improved version of oneself with purpose, prosperity, and inner peace.

> Yesterday I was clever, so I wanted to change the world. Today
> I am wise, so I am changing myself.
> —Rumi

Changing oneself can sound scary! A key concept to understand for people who may think that self-work is inaccessible to them or intimidating, is that you don't become better by wanting to necessarily *change* much of yourself, rather, finding the goodness and potential that already exists within you. Allowing your light to shine from within and the inner possibilities to emerge, is a journey itself. Our *higher self* resides within us, and we need to reveal it bit by bit through shifting inwards.

A lot of the inspiration in this book comes from my Islamic value system and its teachings alongside my coaching trainings and studying human psychology. My work revolves around understanding and conquering the mind and regulating emotions related to everything pertaining to life. With the intention to become a conscious individual, it is very easy to accept the traditional, ethical, or religious knowledge that gets passed down to us, however, truly understanding the shifts that are needed on a much deeper sub-conscious level, is where magic happens.

We are not conditioned to practice our knowledge-based wisdoms as a society. We blindly accept that which is socially or traditionally passed down to us without fully understanding a lot of the reasoning behind. The standards are corrupted, the goals confused, and the pressures are imposed on us at an age where we are unable to question things. And very soon our habits are formed. This is why, as I alluded to earlier, a lot of unlearning must happen before we begin to renew and redesign our truly aligned best life.

The Inner Shift will serve as an easy guide to transform your mindset, master your emotions, heal, and live a more soulfully aligned and peaceful life. You'll learn to set your own individual goals and pursue your own version of success. You'll overcome your past pains and current struggles to design your dream future with a renewed mindset. The positive ripple effects of implementing this work will be seen in all areas of your life.

This book has been an ongoing project which has spanned over three years. As I was halfway through my writing process, we were hit with COVID-19. The times quickly changed into a universal collective need for an internal dialogue while isolated within our homes. Many triggers became apparent, and many patterns were revealed, as quarantine continued. The whole world was suddenly occupied with all the changing regulations and lifestyle adaptations alongside healing on many levels. The overwhelm put a halt on my writing process as it felt somewhat irrelevant.

In the midst of all that, our youngest daughter got diagnosed with an extremely demanding chronic health condition, type 1 diabetes, which made it very difficult for me to continue writing. Times became extremely stressful for our family. I took a break from writing as I needed to process my emotions and allow things to sink in. It was a very sad time to say the least!

As some time passed, I realized that the things I highlight in this book are relevant regardless of the times. No matter what you go through in life, you will always have to return to yourself, your thoughts, your soul. There will always be the need for introspection and going deeper within to find answers. This book will help you through that process.

> *One can have no smaller or greater mastery than mastery of oneself.*
> —*Leonardo da Vinci*

I share my raw and vulnerable stories in this book because I'm human. I don't 'advise' anyone from a place higher above. I'm standing here with you, with all my imperfections, ready to learn and relearn and adapt and grow alongside of you. I truly believe healing happens collectively. Just as we can hurt as a collective, so can we heal. I also grow through my clients' experiences while I work with them. A relatable story can have a profound impact.

We all have more strength, more resilience, and more inner wisdom than we give ourselves credit for. We must make connection with our inner intelligence to transform ourselves and create our own unique impact. This verse below has a powerful message for us all as it explicitly mentions that change must come from within.

> *"Indeed, Allah (God) will not change the condition of a people until they change what is within themselves."*
> —*The Holy Quran (13:11)*

The aim of this project is to nudge the reader to shift their attention and awareness more inwards as opposed to focusing on external stuff. Creating inner strength and confidence to attain contentment intrinsically as opposed to relying on extrinsic factors such as other people, things, situations, or life events. Instead of seeking approvals and happiness from external sources, this work supports you to empower yourself from within, giving you strong authority over your life.

I invite you to gently acknowledge your internal resistance to change and get curious about it. Imagine what your better version might look like. Any amount of change begins with self-compassion and accepting where one stands today. Otherwise, the idea of changing ourselves can be daunting. No matter where you are, you can begin self-work. It is your sacred journey within.

I am extremely grateful to Allah (God) for enabling me to take on such a lengthy project. I want to also extend immense gratitude towards my loving and supportive husband *Rizwan* and my most amazing children, *Ibraheem, Aasiyah, Hafsah*, and *Safiyyah* for always holding me accountable and encouraging me to write this book. I love you all! Thank you for reading many of the chapters and having meaningful deep discussions as a family and helping me through the writing process♡. Additionally, deep gratitude goes to my parents, who raised me well and taught me to aim high. I couldn't have completed this passion project without you all! Anything good here is with God's help and an honour for me, and any shortcomings are my own imperfect attempts.

Enjoy the read!

To be yourself in a world that is constantly trying to make you something else is the greatest accomplishment.

—Ralph Waldo Emerson

Be Yourself

Alife changing principle to adopt is to *be yourself*. You might ask, "Of course I am me! What does that even mean?" Actually, many people don't know who they are, and therefore, struggle to be themselves. Most of our lives are spent pleasing others, chasing after customary merits of happiness, attaining standardized education and occupation to maintain a certain lifestyle, etc. You are taught who to be through your idealistic surroundings. You learn to become uncomfortable with being different. You forget how unique and individualistic you are meant to be. And if you happen to be the *black sheep*, like myself, you try even harder to blend in and lose yourself along the way.

From a young age, we are continuously being programed by our surroundings, aiming towards that goal of attaining acceptance, happiness, and success. As if there is only one right way to be validated as an accomplished being! We are fed a constant ideal to chase after, which we struggle to mold ourselves into, regardless of how unaligned we may feel deep inside.

There are things that make you special and you must show up with all facets of you that make you unique. You've got your own expression, personality, opinions, strengths, passions, and aspirations. If you keep suppressing who you are, you will eventually feel uneasy within yourself and become unfulfilled with your adaptations. You must sit alone a long while with the much-needed thought, *Who am I?* and begin the journey of self-discovery.

Many of us spend a great chunk of our adolescent years confused about our identity as a person: our values, our inclinations, our personality traits. Whatever is popular, becomes acceptable or desirable.

People personify a certain character to carry out a likeable image and strive hard to maintain appearances. The fear of judgement keeps us from showing up as our genuine selves. We dim our light anticipating to 'fit in' or to avoid making others uncomfortable.

We are not generally taught to find or appreciate ourselves for who we are at a younger age. We are labelled and told who to be in order to blend in or be accepted. We are compared to others and criticized for being different. So, as we get older, we get accustomed to wearing masks and hiding our true selves. Many never find the courage to own who they are, feeling lost, which negatively impacts their self-worth. They begin to develop insecurities, fears, limiting self-beliefs, and doubts that keep them small and unfulfilled.

I had a client once share with me how she hated being "socially awkward" and "introverted." Living in a society that appreciates and caters towards an extroverted person, she felt disadvantaged. She wanted to change how she interacted with people and ease up in social situations. She is an introvert yet very opinionated. Besides bringing her awareness to her negative self-judgement, I suggested shifting her perspective and seeing her introversion as an important aspect of who she really was. It was, in fact, her unique attribute as opposed to a problem. Soon she began to see all the ways she enjoyed being an introvert and how she could use it towards her benefit in many situations. She had her big breakthrough and realized that she needed to be who she was rather than trying to change herself. She now loves and regards who she is and works around her individual personality needs.

Our mind is wired to stay safe with the known, it avoids intuition and challenging thoughts. It likes being comfortable with the conditioned limiting beliefs, expectations, and fears. It is safe to just go along with what is familiar and not question things, even if such detachment to our souls' calling might be painful. Our minds' paradigm doesn't always serve us because it wants us to conform to the mainstream and avoid taking risks. It pushes us to follow the trends regardless of the void we may feel inside. In order to discover exciting facts about yourself and your purpose, you must begin to challenge your mind a bit and look beyond what's customary.

Who Are You?

I find it fascinating to uncover the truths about the women I coach. I caught a few of my clients by surprise when I asked them questions like, "Who are you?" or "What are your dreams?" or "What do you wish people knew about you?" or "What are your values?" or "What do you want to leave behind you?" I've witnessed tears, emptiness, silence, and confusion upon challenging women with such questions.

> *The most common ego identifications have to do with possessions, the work you do, social status and recognition, knowledge and education, physical appearance, special abilities, relationships, person and family history, belief systems, and often nationalistic, racial, religious, and other collective identifications. None of these is you.*
>
> —Eckhart Tolle, *The Power of Now: A Guide to Spiritual Enlightenment*

When I ask my clients the question, "who are you?" they are quick to tell me what titles they have been given or what they have achieved or what they do or what happened to them. Things like, "I'm a mom," "I'm a widow," "I'm an accountant," etc. could be your life events or what happened to you or what you do, but they are certainly not your identity. These things don't make you *who* you are. Anything that can change about you or your situation in life should never be attached to your core identity.

It can sound tricky to answer the question "who are you?" but when you start giving it some deep thought, what follows is curiosity, excitement, and a new sense of self-reflection. The most enlightening journey to embark on is the journey to yourself, which introduces you to your own *inner shift*. And the most exciting thing for you is to discover who you really are, as it will then shape your true purpose in life.

Finding Yourself

In order to find who you are, you may need to understand who you currently think you are and question everything you believe about yourself. Some general question that can get you thinking can be:

- What are your core beliefs about your existence?
- How are you gifted?
- Are you introverted or extroverted, and how that plays out for you?
- Do you like to use your imagination or are you factual?
- What are your main fears?
- Do you use logic more or intuition?
- What is your definition of 'success' and why?
- What makes you happy?
- What are your dreams?
- What are your limiting beliefs?
- What needs healing inside of you?
- What is your purpose in life?
- What do you look forward to in the future?

It can be an exciting yet emotional process to really *find yourself*. You get really honest with yourself. You might need to peel some layers and look deeper within. Some masks may need to be removed that you are accustomed to wearing. You may or may not be ready to accept some things about yourself. You get to discover who you are and how you can claim your identity, values, self-beliefs, perceptions and much more.

The thing is, there is no right or wrong kind of personality. You are who you are and there are no judgements on that. Once that process is wholly accepted, I support and teach my clients to love and accept who they are and take pride in themselves. That is where the beautiful journey of *self-mastery* truly begins.

Being unapologetically yourself can significantly grow your self-esteem. You have your signature way of conducting yourself. You have parts of you that you will become proud of once you begin to truly explore yourself. Various dimensions of your life become clear to you based on how you see yourself and the world around you. Your temperaments, insecurities, attitudes, or problems become apparent as you begin to understand what part you play as *who you are* in that point in time. Once you know who you are, you can authentically accept yourself and begin to grow into the better version of you that already exists inside you and needs to be revealed.

Self-Discovery and Self-Esteem

A few years back, as a naive people pleaser, I had a situation that struck me hard and got me started on my self-exploration path. I had to know who I was a bit deeply. I didn't want to feel lost and unaligned. I wanted to live more meaningfully. Somewhere, somehow, I was looking to make someone else happy with me. It takes courage to question things and look a bit harder to find answers within oneself. Instead of worrying about Why am I like this? or What I need to change? I needed to first ask: Who am I?

I embarked on my journey to finding myself a little more keenly in my early thirties. I took any test I could find to see what kind of a person I was. I truly discovered my individuality when I stumbled upon the Myers-Briggs personality test and found out I have an extraverted, intuitive, feeling, and perceiving (ENFP) personality. I have done a lot of research on the testing and absolutely resonate with the test. I was overjoyed with all the revelations that surfaced as I seemed to have many of the answers to the things I wondered about myself and questioned all my life. I began to dig deeper and explored my tendencies and traits in a way I had never before. I became fascinated with the test and researched it thoroughly to educate myself on its scientific accuracy. I also use this test as a tool to help my clients understand themselves better.

We all have our basic tendencies regarding how we process life, however, we are more inclined in some ways than others. None of these tendencies are better or worse, but it is important to recognize and understand them to better develop a holistic understanding of ourselves. For example, I realized that in my immediate family growing up, everyone besides myself was mostly inclined to be a *thinker* yet I am quite the *feeler*, based on the Myers-Briggs test. Discovering just that explained a lot to me.

As a child, I felt the pressure to be a certain way to be accepted as *good enough*. I was labelled as being "too sensitive" when I needed deeper, more meaningful emotional connections. I got hurt easily and I didn't like that. I cried easily and thought it was a problem. I thought I was not smart as I struggled with learning from books, because as a natural artist, I was more of a hands-on and visual learner. I didn't learn much from standard schooling, yet I figured out ways to make good grades. With all righteous intentions in my upbringing, I grew up with wrong concepts about who I needed to be to prove myself. Sadly, on the inside, I felt unappreciated and not "good enough."

It required self-compassion and a non-judgmental curiosity for me to question and understand things for myself. I began to search for different aspects of my individuality. Learning to embrace the fact that I am the only true version of myself was exciting. I was the creative-minded daydreamer. Little did I know, I was wired differently than those I compared myself to. I uncovered my own special talents, intelligence, and intuitive wisdom. And I am not alone! As I connected with likeminded people, I realized many others dealt with similar challenges as myself and yearned to share their gifts.

I decided to minimize the inner self-criticizing chatter and limit what kind of external noise I let in. Slowly, I began to value myself more. I learned to understand my perspectives and feelings without self-judgement. The more I got curious and looked deeper within, the more answers I found. The more I was ready to be *me!*

I fell in love with my newly found self. Not only was I able to embrace my qualities and talents as I enhanced them, I was also able to accept my challenges and shortcomings and was prepared to work on them. I felt perfectly whole and good enough with my *imperfect* self.

Knowing yourself is the beginning of all wisdom.
—Aristotle

Realizing my uniqueness was one thing yet accepting and loving it was another level altogether. And this is true for you! It is true for everyone who is too much for others—too quiet, too opinionated, too sensitive, too nerdy, too hyper, too awkward, too different, too anything! Don't allow anyone to put those labels on you. Block them out! You are you and that is your normal. Own who you are fully and grow that person further.

Finding My Strengths

For me, self-recognition was an ongoing journey that spanned over a few years. The times I felt aligned or disconnected with myself, I noticed my life reflected that. As I connected with my authentic self, I appreciated myself more. The more I understood who I was, the more humility I was able to embody.

I've always been an artist at heart. But I resisted practicing, as I wasn't taught to think much of it more than a "waste of time." For over a decade, I remained detached from my yearning to create art. As I began to draw again in my thirties, it was so natural, so fluent, and rewarding. I became alive. I enjoyed my *me time* and felt relaxed. It was as if I was reviving my spirit through my art. I discovered how naturally abstract ideas came to me as I doodled away freehandedly. I enjoyed the sense of freedom I felt through self-expression. I had no fear of missing out on anything as I connected with my inner longing for practicing what was so natural to me. I would rather be lost in my sacred space creating something magical. I practiced new skills and used various mediums for my art. Pursuing my passion felt more like being myself and I became more confident in my craft.

When I felt brave enough to show the world that perhaps I was gifted as an artist, I quietly launched myself as a henna artist and quickly got recognized as one of the top names in the region. The courage to even allow myself to be called an *artist* was yet another internal struggle, as I was raised to dismiss my artistic inclinations. Appreciating artistic talent in the nineties was not a thing! At least in my surroundings. I began to learn the art of 'breaking the pattern' and challenging the norm.

Claiming my new space and being admired for it was a game changer for my self-worth. It shifted my views on what is valuable and successful in life. The more I pursued my talent and put myself out there, the more opportunities knocked on my door. I also discovered my entrepreneurial tendencies. Although it wasn't an easy ride, being able to create a business out of your passions is one of the most exciting things you can do to live a fulfilled life.

What I learned is that trying things differently and stepping outside of your comfort zone can be your *growth zone*. I always found the passion to teach inside me, so I thought, Why not homeschool our kids? It took a lot of courage and ownership of our values and choices as a family to pursue this path. Being the primary teacher and facilitator, I had a heavy responsibility on me. With God's help, from each setback, and each new lesson, I grew resilient and remained steadfast. Being able to invest time and energy into my children's learning gives me the most satisfaction, regardless of how others judged my choices.

Knowing your strengths is a huge advantage. Once you are aware, you can build on your qualities to create your ideal life. Enhancing your skills and pursuing your passions make you feel accomplished, thereby increasing your self-esteem. It is one of the saddest things to never get to discover your gifts in this life.

Similarly, knowing your weaknesses is extremely important. There is no shame in accepting and working around things you naturally struggle with. When we understand that a true sense of self requires humbly recognizing and working with all aspects of ourselves, we show up authentically.

As I discovered my strong emotional intelligence on a deeper level and became obsessed with self-work, I uncovered my inner-most calling to change lives through coaching others. I had to let go of the idea that I need to be someone perfect before I got into teaching or leading others. Confidence and humility go together. I want to never stop learning. I have a long way ahead of me. I'm ready to make more mistakes, dream more, and ascend to the next best version of myself. One can't ever fully *arrive* on this path as it is ever ongoing. But one can certainly find their strengths and amplify their impact through developing them.

Becoming Authentic

A key intention in finding ourselves is exploring *authenticity*. People are scared to be known as who they are, feeling vulnerable and judged, especially if you're different and find it hard to fit in. We are not prepared to be rejected or disappointed, which is why we remain small and undiscovered at times. In fact, the reality is that being real, open, and vulnerable invites people in and allows them to relate to you on a much deeper and more intimate level. It is hard to make authentic connections when you're looking to blend in and hide your true self.

Most people resort to small talk and refrain from having deeper conversations. In fact, many also fake confidence and pretend to be someone they are not. They are uncomfortable being genuine, pretending to be feelingless and keeping up appearances. We may impress others through our strengths, however, we truly connect with others through sharing our weaknesses. Once we dare to become true to ourselves, we begin to show up more authentically.

> *Daring Greatly means to have the courage to be vulnerable. It means to show up and be seen. To ask for what you need. To talk about how you're feeling. To have the hard conversations.*
>
> —Brené Brown, *Daring Greatly*

It is important to be your true self, knowing that different stages in life require a different version of you. Understanding that every life situation is there to unfold a newer, better version of you. When you are unable to be authentic, you are in denial about something and you blind yourself to the truth, knowing only how you've shown up in the past based on your limitations. Allowing your difficulties to become major blocks can make you feel stuck. Your struggles are your guideposts on the journey of self-discovery, rather than roadblocks.

Authenticity demands the courage to accept mistakes from a past version of yourself. It asks you to discover what is possible as you give a fresher perspective to your experiences. Wisdom is not meant to arrive all at once. Of course, you were who you were because that is all you knew. To become authentic, you let go of victimization and learn to keep a mindful check on your thoughts, words, and behaviours.

By stepping into your authenticity, you automatically come into greater alignment that serves you most. Allowing yourself to have the courage to catch yourself when you are defensive, triggered, or in denial. That is where you will check in with your truth and face your fears and challenges. It's where you will recognize what needs healing and where you need to grow.

Being authentic is your natural way of being. Allow yourself to be who you naturally are. Be the quirky, spontaneous, or funny if that's what your nature calls for. Be the serious, quiet, or gentle if that's how you are naturally comfortable. Be expressive, opinionated, and articulate if you have the gift of excellent speech. Be wise, thoughtful, and inspiring if you like deep connections. Be unapologetically passionate about your values and live your truth, even if it seems strange to others. Just don't hold back or pretend to be like someone else! Your *right* can be someone else's *wrong*, and you must accept that. You are entitled to your perspective, and it may evolve over time. It's when you own every part of *you* is when you begin to connect with your inner-self and build true confidence.

There is so much distraction outside of you. Begin to look inwards and learn interesting things about yourself. Own your individuality. Your contentment with yourself becomes contagious and inspires others to do the same. All personal growth work begins with deeper self-discovery and awareness of who you are today and who you wish to become.

Reflect

1. What part(s) of you are you hiding or are ashamed of? How can you reframe and take pride in them? (i.e., remove the masks).

2. Where do you need work? What needs to heal?

3. What is your ideal image of yourself?

4. What personality type are you? Take the test and uncover many interesting things about yourself at www.16personalities.com.

5. What is one belief you currently hold right now that you don't want to believe about yourself? Is it even true? How would you challenge it?

By not accepting personal responsibility for our circumstances, we greatly reduce our power to change them.

—Steve Maraboli

Quit Playing Victim

How are you showing up in life? Are you blaming everything outside of yourself? Are you complaining, criticizing, avoiding challenges, and living in fear? Are you quick to take offence and are overly defensive? Do you feel like a sufferer who is targeted by others? Could you possibly be playing victim in most situations in life? What does that mean? When we have a victim mentality, we filter our being through an insecure, narrow-minded lens, which is used to perceive other people and the reality of all things.

At times, we truly are victims and need to escape situations or set boundaries. While it's important to claim the role of a victim where we have genuinely been victimized or abused, we cannot live wholesome lives unless we ultimately step out of the victim role and into the responsible and more empowered role.

We all have had times where we felt like it was easy to blame someone else or our situation for whatever wasn't going right. Making excuses and getting out of tough situations seems easier when we can just point fingers towards something outside of us. That is our way of feeling sorry for our situation and negatively *coping* with whatever it is that we feel unsettled about. The problem arises where we choose to attribute all power externally instead of stepping into our own internal resources.

The Big Inner Shift

Like most people, I also had times where I chose a victim mindset in some ways. Although it has not been a constant mindset for me, I have had my taste of it. For example, I became harsh towards myself at times while expressing my inability to accomplish what someone else did. I had my own limiting beliefs that I needed to break through. Whether it was my feelings of incompetence in some ways or lacking the confidence to step into my imperfect genius, I had sub-consciously chosen to make excuses instead of accepting my wonderful self. The more expectations I built upon my comparisons with others, the more there was to blame outside of myself. I needed to tap into my inner self and become consciously aware of what I needed to shift from within.

As I sought personal development and began to focus inwardly, I became aware that my emotional tendencies needed a more logical reflection. Holding high expectations from others, followed by disappointments, was causing me pain. I needed to stop giving others the power to take care of my feelings. I decided to give big-heartedly without expecting anything back. I had to overlook others' shortcomings and focus on myself. Mastering my own thinking and feeling habits became my priority. And more so, I became focused on my goals that were individual to me and incomparable to others'. This *inner shift* freed me and elevated my self-belief.

Why People Feel like Victims

Some people only have a personal victim story here and there, yet a lot of people are too stuck in a *victim mindset* regularly. So much so that it has become an addictive survival mechanism, which can be hard to bring awareness to and overcome. Just like anything else, the first step is understanding what's going on. Many people resort to victimhood based on their preconceived notions about anything they experience. If they have an expectation based on evidence regarding anything that happens to them, especially if they are comparing themselves to the ideals they have in their minds, they may fall into playing the victim.

Sometimes expecting perfection can be the cause to developing a victim mindset. Basically, a victim ends up losing control over life's challenges and resorts to making excuses and assigning blame somewhere outside of themselves. A recipe to disempowering oneself and inviting sadness and failure in life!

A victim acquires a dysfunctional mindset that seeks to feel disadvantaged in order to gain attention or avoid self-responsibility. People who struggle with the victim mentality are convinced that, on some level, life is beyond their control. This limited belief results in blame games and pity parties fuelled by pessimism, fear, or anger. It becomes a toxic way to cope with challenging situations for most people.

You're playing the victim when things don't go your way and you make excuses. You're playing the victim if you feel sorry for yourself or think that it's not your fault. You're playing the victim if you choose to allow people to take advantage of you. You're playing the victim if you don't take responsibility for your part in any unpleasant event. You're playing the victim if you think in absolutes like "always" or "never." You're playing the victim if you don't feel like you have any control over your life or feel stuck emotionally, mentally, or physically. I'm sure you can relate to some of the above. Well, get ready for the ride… it's time to change that!

Outcomes of Victimhood

Self-pity is easily the most destructive of narcotics; it is addictive,
gives momentary pleasure and separates the victim from reality.
—John Gardner

Playing the victim does have a few addictive incentives, which makes it very difficult to break out of, such as: not having to take responsibility for anything, getting to be right all the time, people feeling sorry for you, enjoying gossiping and entertaining others, feeling the right to be upset with others, and feeling *safe* from being guilty. Although all that doesn't heal you, it may help you cope in a negative way. These may seem like benefits to most victims, but are they really?

A victim's false sense of validation and attention-seeking behaviour can provide some satisfaction momentarily, however, it leaves you with disempowering negative consequences, such as feeling codependent and helpless. It keeps you small and prevents you from personal growth and fulfilment. You become addicted to expecting others' approvals while building animosity, inviting drama, and wasting time and energy. You may end up manipulating others and cause self-deception, which is inauthentic and distances you from yourself. You might find people distancing away from you because of your toxic behaviour and negative energy. Besides, all the time wasted while complaining, blaming others, and self-pity meltdowns can never be justified.

A victim may perceive that other people are out to get them or have some kind of an agenda against them, losing trust and peace of mind. You keep overthinking and ruminating about past events, reliving your old pain again and reinvesting emotions that disempower you further. Your victimizing attitude limits you and sabotages you, keeping you vulnerable and unhappy. It's a mental trap! But don't worry! It's never too late to shift your mindset and reclaim your power.

How to Shift into Your Power?

I want you to know that no one is born with a victim mentality. Instead, it is an acquired personality trait as a result of early-life conditioning and coping mechanisms. This is good news, because whatever is an acquired trait can also be unlearned and changed. Although most of such traits are acquired by us as children and are beyond our control, it is our responsibility as adults to step into our power and reclaim responsibility for our lives. We can have life-transforming breakthroughs, which lead up to an empowering paradigm, in the process.

The secret is to shift into the *creator mode*, where we challenge ourselves, evolving and spiraling upwards, so we can proceed with clarity and confidence. To enhance our creative ability, we must get to work. We can't throw our hands up in the air obliviously and seek sympathies from others. We truly want to change this vicious cycle of victimhood that hardens our hearts and incapacitates us. Knowing that something needs to shift within us is imperative for any positive action to follow.

Let's affirm this right now: *We are not victims!* Things are not just happening to us without control. To gain control over your story, choose to be the *victor* in your life as opposed to the *victim*. We play a significant role in attracting the reality of what our lives look like. It can be easy to simply blame and complain. But that is not how we create a powerful story. It defeats us and the cycle repeats until we shift.

Life will bring an assortment of tests for everyone. We can give up and operate on a reactive self-pity mode or take the power into our own hands. We can choose to take control of our lives to change our life story. As the main character of our life story, we get to choose to be the protagonist, the hero whose story is worth sharing with others. And that will take the courage to shift your mindset and search for answers.

When unexpected difficult things happen in life, acceptance of *what is* and really prioritizing your own healing will pave the path forward and allow you to become a part of the solution. It is a very conscious choice to move on from draining emotions such as despair, or self-pity. The magic lies in truly knowing that you can feel better through rewiring your brain to think differently. In most cases, all that is required is shifting your perspective and seeing things from a different lens altogether. Instead of thinking, Why me? you can think: What can I do now? or What does this teach me?

When you change the way you think, you'll learn to self-validate and self-regulate and ask for help when you need it. Instead of *waiting to be rescued*, you will shift into your power to respond in a way that helps your growth and recovery. You can reject things assertively, set healthy boundaries, eliminate things that drain you, avoid what doesn't benefit you, invest where you need improvement, instill self-discipline, and shift your ways of thinking to align with whatever you wish to create. *You are not a victim unless you choose to be*. Period.

Let's choose wiser. And yes, I'm not going to lie, it can be difficult for you if playing the victim is all you've known, and this has been your way of being for a very long time. Some of my clients have told me, "This is what I've seen in my family." As if they don't know any different way to be. I tell them, "This is where you get to break the cycle instead of repeating a destructive pattern that may get passed down to your coming generations."

You may need some healing work. You may need to forgive yourself. You may need a lot more courage to accept difficult things about yourself. You may need to build your self-esteem and gain the courage to be honest with yourself. This can require a lot of inner work. But you keep challenging yourself in different ways until your become solid on the inside, and that is the only way you consistently show up going forward.

Ways to Overcome Victimhood

You can just start by writing down ways you blame things outside of yourself regularly, to gain some clarity around your thinking patterns. You need to use non-judgement and self-compassions for this process. There is a fine line between compassion and a victim mentality. When you are choosing to heal yourself and cure your resentments, you choose self-compassion. You validate yourself and allow some difficult feelings to pass through you as you learn to develop new ways of thinking and feeling.

We need to shift our mindset as we take ownership and live a more fulfilling life. Most people are reactive. They go through life unconsciously reacting to things that go on, feeling powerless as a result of what's on the news, the weather, their job, traffic, or even the way they get treated in relationships. The reality is that you have an incredible power to create and shape the reality around you. You can consciously set the scene to suit your needs. You can choose how you respond to things and what you think, say, feel, or do. Here are some tips for you to overcome playing the victim in life:

- Make a strong intention and set a sincere goal to overcome you habit of playing victim. Only when you seriously commit to changing, will you invest time and energy towards taking action.

- Everything begins in your mind, always. As Buddha says, *"Our life is the creation of our minds."* Prime your mind with positive thoughts and affirmations. For example, "I am responsible for my life" or "I am empowered to create change." It will help reprogram your subconscious mind.

- Avoid complaining. Try a challenge to shift out of your victim mentality and commit to a period of 'no complaining.' And by that, I mean no gossiping, blaming, or whining.

- Switch your focus to solutions and positive responses. Instead of thinking, I can't do anything about it, say to yourself, I'll find a way.

- Avoid oversharing with others. The more evidence you create for your victimhood, the lesser you'll be in control.

- Ask yourself the right questions. Instead of asking, Why me? or, Why are people are so difficult? ask yourself: Why did this happen? What can I learn from this situation? How can I avoid this in the future? And voila! You'll be shifting into *creative mode* from a previously known *reactive* one.

- Let go of unwanted feelings to make room for creativity. Release negative emotions of guilt, hate, anger, and self-pity because they keep you in captivity and reinforce your identity as a victim. Forgive those who have hurt you. (Refer to the chapters "Let Go" and "Forgive.")

Remember, shifting how you think in life is a slow process and it can take a lot of practice. The more you are aware and willing, the quicker you'll notice yourself evolve into the person who is more in charge of your life. If you keep thinking that your solutions to life problems exist outside of you, then you lose your power. What you seek externally is most definitely *within* you.

Reflect

1. What are some ways in which you currently play a victim?
2. What can you change to take your power back?
3. How will you gain responsibility as opposed to reactivity?

*The price of greatness
is responsibility.*

—Winston Churchill

Take Responsibility

In our household, this was a big lesson I remember as a child. We were not allowed to make excuses, blame anyone, or miss opportunities. I remember my dad repeating "No ifs, no buts" quite often. I'm not sure I soaked in all the advice at that time. It was intimidating as a child, but somehow it programed me on a deeper level. I'm able to absorb the useful messaging from my younger days now. I recognize why my dad became the person he did from practicing his strong principles. He doesn't blame anyone for his life and takes full responsibility for whatever happens in his life. But this lesson came to my understanding after growing up and finding my own way.

As a society, not many of us are taught to take responsibility for our lives. We always see complaints about destiny, the system, the people in authority, our genes, parents, environment, life events, etc. As a result, we learn to give up control and be on the mercy of a system, family, our luck etc. and get programed to think and act in powerless ways. If you want to be empowered and take control of your life, you must learn to take full responsibility for your life. It will tweak your paradigm in a way that allows more clarity, problem solving, and authority over your life. The antidote for the *victim mindset* discussed in the previous chapter, is *taking responsibility*.

Life isn't something that happens to us, rather something we shape and control. With the onset of unannounced events that are entirely out of our control, the outcomes that relate to our happiness and inner peace are entirely dependent on how we respond. When experiencing hardships, one may be inclined to feel discouraged and helpless. However, it's important to remember that we can be mindful of our choices that can significantly shape our experience positively. Accepting what we can't change and changing what we can.

A lack of responsibility for your life may show up as pessimistic thinking, inability to accomplish things, unfavorable results, a victimized mentality, frequent arguments, confusion, complaining attitude, lack of resolution, stagnancy, and unfulfillment. When we become responsible for our lives, we notice more things going in our favour. If you want to create a better quality of life, filled with peace and joy, then you must be mindful of how you approach the way you live your life.

Shifting the Attitude

Taking responsibility doesn't mean blaming yourself for your circumstances. Rather, it is using your own power and agency to turn things in your favour, regardless of what happens or who causes things. This requires an attitude that prepares you to face life head on, with all its challenges, knowing that it may be difficult, but there is a way that will work for your greatest good. You must be willing to take charge, like a shepherd is to his sheep and a captain is on a ship. You are the captain of your life!

A common trait of irresponsible people is that they find an array of excuses. A person who wants to lose weight, eat healthier, or exercise may say that they can't because they don't have time. However, if they are to be responsible, accountable, and honest, they would be able to figure out a way to make time. You can find many reasons not to make life changes. Remember, that is your choice.

We must begin by confronting ourselves about the lies we tell ourselves. Things like; I can't change myself, God made me like this, It's my fate, Others have caused me to become this way, This is all that I have known, etc. With such a debilitating mindset, we can never take responsibility for our lives or entertain any new exciting ideas. The moment we understand that we can play a key role in creating our destiny, regardless of anything that is meant to happen to us outside of our control, we can generate space for contentment and success.

The key mindset we need to begin any amount of inner work is that *we are fully responsible for our lives.* Imagine how empowering that belief is! How courageous and in control one feels! Human experience is caused from an internal force within. You can be at peace with a simple life and extremely unhappy living luxuriously in a castle. What's within you ultimately matters. Taking your power back is the key. Of course, with that intention, we can bring our attention towards what needs to shift within us in order to make space for all the goodness that follows.

To change your life, you need to change yourself. Either you change how you think, how you experience your feelings, how aware you choose to become, and what actions you are willing to take consistently to keep on evolving. It is called *the law of paying the price.* You can't get better on accident. Any self-improvement is intentional work. Believe that you have the potential to change yourself for the better. Ultimately, it is not what you have, rather, who you are in life, that truly matters. Because that creates your inner worth. Your true abundance is in developing yourself.

Owning Your Choices

When I was younger, in my teenage years and even partially in my early twenties, I relied heavily on others' opinions and approvals. I looked for agreeability, cooperation, and opinions of others before taking decisions. I let fear of rejection limit me. I took lesser risks and struggled with low self-confidence. I remember wanting to feel accepted by my friends and falling into peer pressure through childhood and my teens. At times, I didn't seem to have an opinion or preference. For the most part, I felt like life was happening to me and I had no control over things. Taking responsibility seemed scary and unimaginable as I wasn't ready to be who I was.

Evidently, as I grew older, I learned to value my individuality and favour my choices. I learned to own my deep values and allowed them to surface. A major turning point in my life was when I began to become more religious. I questioned why I called myself a Muslim and how that identity played out in my life. Upon doing extensive research and allowing Allah (God) to guide my way, I found peace in practicing the beautiful teachings of Islam. I wanted to take the hijab (head scarf) for my own self-expression and as a symbol of my conviction to my faith. My dad was not in agreement with my decision at first, but after the initial shock, he let me be. It was very challenging for me to go against his consent. Although I sensed his disapproval at times, I could tell one thing for a fact: he was proud of my courage!

Over time, I felt like my dad accepted my bold decision to unapologetically practice my faith. After all, when we depict strength in our actions, it is praiseworthy whether others agree with us or not. He has no idea what his unspoken approval had done for me. This was my first time going against his will in a big way. It liberated me, strengthened me, and allowed me to explore and discover things I could never imagine. Just because I learned to take responsibility for my own choices. I developed the courage to listen to what I wanted for myself and find my own path.

Taking responsibility for our choices in life is important as we become adults. Many people get stuck in their old patterns, which makes it difficult for them to own their choices. In my adulthood, the more I relied on myself for my decisions in life, the more I was able to own the outcomes. Had I put all that power in the hands of those around me, I would have held them partly accountable for the outcomes as well. Taking decisions with full awareness and responsibility will always make you feel like a winner.

In 2008, when it was time for our little guy to begin formal learning, my husband and I took the *risky* decision to homeschool our children. It is not something most people accepted or understood back then. Though, after living through *Covid times*, we have a lot more awareness now as it has become a highly desirable choice, and even a privilege. But when we started off on this journey, it was quite the odd thing to do.

Most people among our family and friends were doubtful for the first few years. With very little support, we gathered the courage and took the leap with many unknowns. It was quite tough in the beginning, however, with much dedication, and a lot of responsibility, came success. People began to ask me for advice on parenting and homeschooling. This journey provided us with some major opportunities for growth, especially because we followed through with what we thought was best for our family. Had we never explored this *unknown* path, we would never expand in ways we did through owning our choice. We got to write our own unique story, worthy of sharing with pride.

Question Your Ownership

Do you ever wonder about how your choices and actions design your life? Or do you simply assume that your life is the way it is by accident? Many things in life are determined by destiny, however, we have a lot of control. We are dealt our set of cards that we get to play our own way, which gives us utmost freedom of choice. Every life situation comes with a hidden message for us to unpack. That is how we find purpose and answers in life's complex journey.

When I coach my clients to overcome anything challenging, I often ask the question, "What role are you playing in this situation?" As they begin to question their ownership in any unhappy situation, the solution begins to reveal itself. One thing to ask yourself is: "Am I *reacting* or *responding*?"

We can take responsibility for everything we do in life. Our health, how we manage our time, our money spending habits, our temperaments, our attitudes, our lifestyle choices, our relationships, and our goals. You see, you attract who you are! So, if you have a lot of drama in your life, well check and see what's your part. If you have relationship issues, see what you bring to the table. If you are failing miserably at achieving something, see what your day looks like and what your habits are. If you exhibit toxic patterns in your interactions, see where you can heal. If you are unhappy with the kind of people surrounding you, see why and how you are allowing them into your life? Once you become brutally honest and begin to take responsibility for your part, you take more power in your hands to solve anything in life. Everything becomes figure-out-able!

I am passionate about helping women understand how much power they actually have in their lives. In my coaching sessions, I encourage my clients to fully own their part. From there, we work on how to master our minds and emotions in order to feel empowered to tackle any situation. Most of the times, the much-needed shift we need to work on, is exploring what is within our control and asserting ourselves accordingly.

> *Look at the word responsibility . . . "response-ability" . . . the ability to choose your response. Highly proactive and successful people recognize that responsibility and take ownership of it.*
> —Stephen R. Covey, *The 7 Habits of Highly Effective People* (Covey 2020)

There are good and bad things that happen to us in life. Life presents itself with its many shades. We can't just accept the good and reject/complain about the bad. The good (blessings, achievements, opportunities) allows us to feel grateful or proud and the bad (setbacks, challenges, disappointments, etc.) teaches us lessons and becomes our benchmark for growth. If you are finding yourself complaining about your situation and making excuses for not achieving a particular goal, you need a mind-shift!

Your setbacks have something to do with you. Your miseries and your sufferings are also your choice. It is how you choose to define things for yourself and whether you allow room for growth and expansion or not. How you respond to whatever comes your way depends on how much control you are ready to claim. For example, choosing to draw closer to God through patience and prayer in calamity allows expansion of the soul. It is always available for you to claim.

You are responsible for your attitude towards life. Being lazy or passive is not an option if you want a successful life. The way you treat yourself and your family shows how responsible you are. How you take care of your health, whether you exercise, what you eat, where you spend time, how much you read, who your friends are, how you raise your children, what you believe, and how much you practice what you know, are all your responsibility.

Taking Personal Responsibility

There are many ways to take personal responsibility for your life that mostly originate from how you think. Start with these ideas:

- Make yourself a priority. You first must feel worthy of a good life to make better decisions. Grow your self-esteem by investing time and energy in pursuing your personal goals.

- Notice your excuses. Think about your limiting beliefs or habits that are keeping you irresponsible. What is holding you back and what do you need to breakthrough?

- Take action. This is probably the most critical part of taking responsibility for your life. Thinking positively is not enough. Take small steps forward towards your goals and stay consistent.

- Choose your company wisely. Distance yourself from complainers, blamers, and people who make excuses for their lives. You are responsible for the kind of influence you invite into your life. Be with those who inspire and encourage you.

Taking Responsibility in Relationships

Many of our setbacks as adults come from our lack of taking responsibility in relationships. If we use our emotional intelligence, we begin to understand that how people *feel* impacts how they *react*. Most people justify how they feel based on their judgements of others' actions towards them. Blaming our emotions on someone else is easy but it doesn't help us. Taking responsibility for our emotional experience gets us free of the blame game.

What is the *blame game*? It is the response we have when someone says or does something that triggers us in a negative way. It is giving up our own power and claiming victimhood. It is giving someone else the power to impact our emotions. Understand that finding someone else to blame in any situation doesn't solve the problem; it only cultivates anxiety and helplessness. By choosing to take responsibility, you do yourself the favour of encouraging growth and acceptance rather than stagnation and suffering. You must focus on understanding your own responses instead of wanting to blame others, as you have no idea where others are coming from.

An example in my own life is when someone's negative attitude bothered me. I kept letting myself build resentment and hurt around that dynamic, wanting to "fix" something. My own understanding was that this person was hating on me and misrepresenting me behind my back. As much as that might have been true, I later learned that their negativity was coming from a place within them. It had nothing to do with me. Perhaps this individual felt insecure, jealous, threatened, or had their own blame story going on against me. Their story didn't have to make sense to me. I just needed to learn how to make peace within myself.

I began to make excuses for others and took back my power through retelling my mind a new story. A story that made me wonder, with compassion, whether a difficult person had more layers within themselves that made them bitter towards happy people. You never know why people behave a certain way when they try to hurt someone else. What happens within them can be intriguing but it's not my business. I also decided to not allow others' behaviours to impact my emotions too much. If I show up authentically and from a place of security, I let go of everything else. Instead, I decided to work on myself and figure out my own inner game, which can be complex enough!

Don't allow other's behaviours to destroy your inner peace. This *inner peace* is not given to you, rather, it is cultivated ever so mindfully. You will heal very quickly when you understand that in any tough situation, whatever internal difficult place anyone comes from is their problem and not yours. People must be responsible for their triggers. Know your own triggers, so you can self-reflect and not project onto others. Instead of reacting based on your triggers, choose to respond more mindfully. This requires awareness and inner work, which is how we take responsibility in any situation.

Empower Yourself

If we want to take responsibility for our lives, we must remove blame. Removing blame in relationships means, not assigning responsibility to anyone for what you experience. It is easy to see the cause-and-effect relationship of someone's behaviour impacting our emotional experience. In reality, the way you experience things is entirely different from how some other person does. No one has that much power to know how intensely their words/actions will impact you. What you interpret may not be what someone else intended. They are being them, and you are holding the emotion by choice. You need to be conscious of how much you allow others to impact you. The more you own your part, the more empowered you become.

A beautiful awakening to keep close to heart is that all pain, failure, and trauma come in our lives as our guides to help us grow wiser and more resilient. Most such trials have to do with other people in our lives. We must intentionally reflect and tweak our lens. If we are open to extracting whatever good there is in any situation, then it is a new opportunity. We could choose blame and self-pity, or allow growth and transformation. It is entirely up to us.

When triggered in relationships, how can we empower ourselves emotionally? It can be difficult not to blame someone else for making us feel bad. We naturally want to justify our behaviour and blame others for their part. Our responses are lead by how we feel. What does it mean to take responsibility for our feelings?

For me, it is creating the new belief that whatever I'm feeling comes from me and not from someone else. It is my personal experience. This manifests in our relationships profoundly. It will allow you to be vulnerable and express how you feel without blaming anyone for your personal emotions. Your feelings are entirely yours and their emotions are valid as well.

If all humans had the consciousness to support each other's emotions all the time, it would have been a wonderful expectation and the outcomes would be ideal. But sadly, that is not a reasonable expectation and therefore, we must build self-reliance.

As you're reading this you might be thinking, Sometimes people say mean things. Should I just let them misbehave towards me and blame myself for feeling hurt? No, of course not! Defend yourself where needed. Distance yourself from hurtful behaviour. Fight back where appropriate. This is also part of being responsible as you guard yourself. However, know that their mean behaviour is not the cause of your hurt. The way you think about people's behaviours causes you to feel a certain way. How you interpret and experience what is happening in your life is always on you. Remember that there are a lot of things in life that are not your fault but are your responsibility. Choose to be a part of the solution in your path forward.

Also, if applicable, take responsibility for your contribution to the event prior to someone upsetting you. This is hard for me personally, because I am my own worst critic at times, and it causes me pain to overthink such events and understand my mistakes. By the end of it, I do learn things for the better. This can take some processing time and it is by no means an easy thing to work on.

Setting boundaries is always important. Blaming is not a way to set a boundary with someone though. Any conflict can be worked out when the person is not put on the defensive for being blamed. The process of conflict, acknowledgement, empathy, and solution is much smoother than conflict, blame, hurt, and shutdown (what I see much of the time, which only leads to a battle of egos).

Taking responsibility is not about waiting to be rescued. Rather, it is about self-validating, self-regulating, asking for help, healing, and going through difficult situations without trying to dodge the process.

Ways to Take Relational Responsibility

Taking responsibility for your part is a courageous and empowering decision. Here are some ways you can practice:

- Empower your thoughts. Create an intention that you affirm to yourself each day, such as, *Today, I will take responsibility for whatever happens in my interactions*. Any new beliefs you create for yourself become your new reality.

- Watch your words. Notice when you use blaming language rather than the language of responsibility. Accountability plays a huge part in self-discipline. Hold yourself accountable by keeping a reflective journal.

- Be mindful of your emotional triggers. Take time to process situations and to respond. Being mindful allows us to have more freedom to choose how to respond more wisely rather than reacting from habit.

- Analyze how different the outcomes of any situation can be once you take responsibility. Any situation can shift based on how empowered you show up.

Reclaim your power through taking full responsibility in your personal as well as social life. When faced with problems, think about your contribution and how can you take your power back? When hit with any tough life situation outside of your control, think about what is the wisest way to respond? Many times, the answer to such situations is choosing acceptance and submission with humility. That can be a very responsible choice!

Reflect

1. What can you start doing to take responsibility in your life right now?
2. How will that transform you mentally or emotionally?
3. Who's help can you ask for?
4. What are some action steps for you?

The difference between greatness and mediocrity is often how an individual views a mistake.

—Nelson Boswell

Accept Your Mistakes

We don't like the idea of making mistakes. I remember especially when I was young, I was brought up to be hard on myself. I hated making mistakes even while I did schoolwork as a child. Trying my hardest to achieve top marks and being sad when sometimes my best was only an 80%. I had to have the best handwriting, so I ripped off the whole page for making a simple mistake while doing homework. I wasted so much time worrying and stressing about littlest things during a time I should have fully enjoyed making all the mistakes a child is only expected to make! I was being conditioned to build an unsettling mindset that required me to have high expectations of myself and not accept less than a known, desired standard.

I think as a child, back in the eighties, we were raised with the messaging that mistakes were shameful and unacceptable. I was not taught the essential concept that I was allowed to, in fact, *supposed to* make mistakes. I always feared *not being good enough* in my attempts to be accepted. I strived for perfection more than excellence, understanding, learning, and simply enjoying the process.

I had always known I was an artist, but it took me too long to trust my artistic inclinations enough to build a small business for myself due to my fear of failure. The first few years after starting my small business were filled with trial and error. I had to make my mistakes to learn all the lessons I wouldn't have learned any other way. Any successful entrepreneur will also tell you this, because any level of success comes to them through making some mistakes.

You simply can't have it all figured out in life, relationships, business, or parenting from the get-go. Accepting that mistakes are a part of the journey is a much-needed, self-compassionate way of thinking to allow further growth. As I let go of my irritation against making mistakes and practiced acceptance, I began to enjoy taking risks and cherished my overall journey with all its imperfections.

You Are Not Your Mistakes

> If you want to grow, you need to get over any fear you have of making mistakes.
> —John C. Maxwell

Making mistakes is a normal part of life. Taking responsibility and facing up to our mistakes are great ways to learn and to avoid repeating them. When you make a mistake, keep in mind that it doesn't mean anything about who you are as a person. Try not to jump to conclusions about your worth. No matter how much someone else tries to associate your mistakes to you, you must detach yourself from your mistakes. Because that is how you'll create room for growth. Nobody's perfect. *You make your mistakes; they don't make you!* (I heard that on a podcast!) Just avoid making the same mistakes repeatedly. Instead, make newer ones to learn new things.

Many times, I convince my clients that they are not the problem. *The problem* is the problem! You have to be the one that works to solve your problems. And this concept is important to embody. Don't take on any labels due to your mistakes. Your mistakes don't define you; they refine you.

Mindset Shift

We must learn to shift our perspective on making mistakes. Accepting that mistakes are inevitable and essential part of the process can help us grow tremendously. Accept that things may go wrong unexpectedly or mistakenly and develop the courage to gracefully become better. Just embracing our own mistakes and life's unpleasant surprises, allows us to face the challenging outcomes. As we dare to expand our comfort zones to achieve more than the ordinary, we go in with the mindset that mistakes are going to happen, and we accept that they will be a vital part of our journey.

Most intelligence develops through making mistakes. After all, it was upon falling over again and again as a toddler that we learned how to stand on our own two feet! Imagine if we gave up after the first few times and felt ashamed for falling. As our nature suggests, our mistakes must be seen as an opportunity to learn and improve, instead of lack of ability.

Many people make mistakes and don't know how to cope with them. If you're ruminating on your mistakes and it's getting you down, learn how to accept what's happened and move forward with grace, rather than dwell on the past. I used to lose sleep and beat myself down for making mistakes. I had to heal the part of myself that yearned to be perfect. I had to look within, ask tough questions, do the difficult inner work, and face my fears. And once I let go of all that held me back and kept me stuck, I felt relieved. I began to draw lessons for myself through making mistakes.

Coach John Wooden summarized how to deal with mistakes best: "A mistake is valuable if you do four things with it: recognize it, admit it, learn from it, forget it." (Wooden n.d.)

Let me share the valuable breakdown here for you to reflect on:

- We must be able to realize our mistakes. If we are unable to recognize our mistakes, then we could be in great loss. Just imagine never becoming aware of your mistakes and trying to prove always being right. How difficult and foolish would that be?

- Being in denial about our shortcomings can lead to defensiveness and insecurity. It can also make us very inauthentic in how we conduct ourselves. Know that making mistakes is a very human thing to allow.

- Be sure to not blame others for your mistakes because you would never be able to fix something you can't own.

- Focus on what lessons can be derived from the mistake. Work alongside someone to help you overcome feelings of shame/guilt. Reframe your mistake purposefully.

- Once the lesson is learned, get over your mistake. Let it out of your system. It has done its job! Only refer to it as helpful data.

Mistakes with Others

When you make mistakes with other people involved, be sure to understand and accept your part and make amends. Communicate, apologize, decide to change for the better, and move on. Sometimes, we are unable to accept our mistakes with others as we fear their judgement and confrontation. We fear that they may not understand us and so we decide to distance ourselves instead. We avoid them and become awkward. This causes more tension between relationships.

Listen! As long as you have to deal with other people in life, you must know that they will never get you at all times and neither will you. Even with all good intentions, you will make mistakes and so will they. People in your life do understand that you are human and will make mistakes. Any relationship has to overcome problems and sort out mishaps wisely. With proper communication, things will resolve. With troublemakers, be cautious and know when to keep a healthy distance.

As we learn to accept our mistakes, we get to grow our *acceptance muscle* in other situations as well. We grow vulnerability and are able to authentically give our best to any given situation. We learn to accept things that come our way that we didn't prepare for and are able to respond with composure and grace. As well, we are gracious and kinder towards others' mistakes and are gentle with them instead of judgemental.

Mistakes are our teachers in life. If you are not making enough mistakes, you are not living enough! We become more interesting and relatable due to our blunders and the lessons we can share. Life is about evolving, so our mistakes can be milestones for us to progress. Start to own and accept your mistakes and feel grateful for what they teach you in life.

Reflect

1. Think about a mistake you made in life that you regret.

2. What steps can you take to accept your mistake and reframe it in a way that you don't regret it anymore? Instead, you are happy it taught you a much-needed life lesson.

3. Try repeating this sequence for another challenging life event.

4. What mistake are you terrified to make?

5. How could making such a mistake possibly grow you?

Expectations were like fine pottery. The harder you held them, the more likely they were to crack.

—Brandon Sanderson, The Way of Kings

Lower Your Expectations

Our expectations determine our reality in many ways. We tend to have high expectations from our lives as well as others because we idealize perfect outcomes. Due to our fear of failure, we have the idea that we need to aim for the best possible results. We often tend to go into situations with a false *entitled* mindset. We expect things to be how we imagine them to be in our minds. Most our false expectations are regarding our idealistic lives and other people. For the sake of our personal growth, we must begin to take a closer look at what we expect in all situations. Our false expectations can lead to constant disappointment in life.

Why do we expect that we can't mess up? Why do we expect others to behave towards us a certain way? Why do we expect that things would go as we planned? Why do we expect our children to always achieve exceptional grades in school? Why do we expect to check off boxes based on a certain timeline? And I can go on and on . . .

We have a distorted idea of what we think we deserve, from life and from others. We are accustomed to expecting our outcomes based on how much effort we put in, or what age we are, our relationship status, what experiences we have been through, or what we know. We expect that our life will evolve according to our plan and that people will behave in predictable ways. We feel secure with the sense of control we create with having high expectations, as the unknown may be scary. Believe me, my ego also likes to fight for control. But this control is an illusion, and it can have serious consequences.

Where do our expectations come from? Our society plays a huge part in shaping our expectations. Our upbringing and experiences could be at play. Sticking to our comfort zones, because they keep us safe and allow us to predict things, can also build specific expectations. And, of course, our *entitled ego* loves to push us to extremes, and expecting certain outcomes is at times the ultimate fantasy.

You may not be aware, but the list of your predetermined expectations can be long. Ask yourself if you're expecting these things:

- Life to always be in your favour.
- "Success" to look the same for you as someone else.
- People to understand and agree with you or like you.
- To have what you think you deserve from situations and people.
- People to reciprocate your acts of goodness.
- People to support you and be there for you when you need.
- To always have health and wealth.
- To never witness grave losses.
- Things to go as planned and be in control.
- Your children to be high achievers and fulfill your dreams.

Expectations From Ourselves

We all plan things to be a desired way and expect certain things from ourselves. But inevitably, at some point in life, we will end up frustrated or disappointed when our plans don't become our desired reality. We may end up feeling like we are not living up to our potential. We might suffer from something like an "expectation hangover." Many of our unrecognized or unfulfilled expectations from ourselves in life can cause distress. And most of the time, our definition of *success* can also be inauthentic and something we don't understand fully.

There is no other *you* in this world. The traits, talents, and opportunities you have available to you are not the same as anyone else's. Accept your unique package as a gift and make the best of your situations without comparing to others and expecting similar results as others. With an open and accepting mind, you will learn to enjoy the process that is unique to you alone. You are the main character in your story, not anyone else's. Your journey is special and unlike anyone else's. You might take longer at things you struggle with at times and where your talents are strong, you will surprise yourself. When you don't expect things to happen a certain way, you give freedom and time to yourself to explore, experiment, make mistakes, try again, learn, and grow.

Many things became clear to me as I learned this lesson in my own life. Anytime I relied on people for my happiness, or lead by fear of disappointment, imperfection, or rejection, I was at loss. As I learned more about my individual goals and personal capacity, my perspective began to change remarkably. We all have our own stamina for things, our unique challenges, needs, and temperaments. And success also can look differently for different people. You can excel at something quickly, which may be challenging for others and vice versa.

We need to discard the idea of being in comparison with others, as the automatic program runs this pattern from childhood. There should be standards, goals, and personal targets that one meets to continually excel in life. However, there is no race to anywhere, but a journey to oneself. There is no perfect relationship, but a good one. There is no perfect outcome or timeline, but one that you mindfully construct for yourself.

Your expectation should only be what is truly aligned with where you are at any point. In doing so, your focus shifts towards enjoying the process instead of being fixated on outcomes. You also gracefully allow for mistakes, imperfections, hurtful surprises, and sadness. And you'll find that you surrender to such setbacks with much humility and ease when you let go of ideal expectations. And let's not forget, those expectations were *only* ideal in your mind!

Having lower expectations doesn't mean you don't aim high. Rather, when you accept that things can go wrong at times, you take more risks and try new things without much fear or worry. You enjoy the feeling of having tried something instead of worrying too much about the possible unpleasant outcome. It helps you overcome *perfectionism* and allows you to truly enjoy achieving your goals. When we are fixated on our ideals of success and keep worrying about what's next, we lose the joy in where we happen to be at present. Letting go of our obsession with the ideals allows us to enjoy the journey more.

Expectations in Relationships

In relationships, the old version of me expected others to reciprocate my big-heartedness. I expected them to understand my ideas and validate me. To defend and support me. I expected them to love me back with the same level of intensity. I justified my feelings by yet another expectation that they should know me as a person and treat me accordingly.

But then, after heartbreaks, misunderstandings, and disappointments, I learned my lessons. It was foolish of me to expect all these things from others, even from those I considered to be close to me. With time, we must realize that we can't expect our particular situations to be in accordance with our perfect imaginations.

A major shift happened in my attitude when I decided to lower my expectations of someone dear to me. I began to make excuses for them instead of believing in reasons why they were wrong according to me. I understood that they also have a perspective that serves them and explains their choices and behaviours. Going even further, and not expecting them to reciprocate me understanding them by understanding me back! I learned to still love them at a distance and be a well-wisher from afar. This shift in my perspective empowered me and allowed me to just do my best and not judge anyone else's actions. Everyone has their journey, and we must honour it as much as our own.

I am still work in progress, so I know I will be presented with new challenges. I am working on cultivating self-assurance and allowing people to misunderstand me. I do get triggered of course, just like anyone else. But my mind works differently now. Instead of asking, How could they do this? or Why did they have to say that? or That was so hurtful, I now ask myself things like, What can I learn here? and What was my mistake? and How can I avoid a situation like this next time? Or What can I forgive? That is a big shift in what I can now expect from my challenging situations.

> *When you expect too much from others, expect to be disappointed.*
> *Rather than laying blame, manage your expectations.*
> —Mufti Ismail Menk

Expecting others to behave in certain situations how *you* would, is going to lead to disappointment for *you*. They won't even be bothered because they were unaware of your expectation. Try to mindfully be neural. You do you and allow others to be them and accept that. Never completely rely on other people for your satisfaction. No one knows exactly what you want from them. No one completely understands what you are thinking and feeling. Even if you communicate your expectation very well (according to *your* understanding), they might not quite understand what exactly is required. And that is because we all have a unique paradigm. How we perceive things can be significantly different from the next person we engage with. No one entirely sees things the way you do. Isn't that mind blowing? This is enough information for us to lower our expectations of others.

As my younger self, I desired happy harmonious relationships. When I got disappointed by others, I blamed either myself or wanted to "fix" something. I came to realize that most my disappointments were due to my high expectations. And that is particularly true for most highly sensitive individuals. We require more attention and validation. But as I brought awareness to this fact, I realized that I needed to lower my expectations. I had to let go of my fixed ideals and began to see how challenging situations served my higher good. What appeared to be emotionally hurtful tests for me, became my priceless teachings. The quality of my relationships evolved as I learned to think differently and began to reframe things positively.

Expectations from Our Children

If you understand the mindset of immigrant parents from third-world countries, you'll know what expectations look like for them! Some parents tend to have the most outrageous expectations from their children. Now I know this pressure is seldom felt in the western cultures, but believe me, it is a very serious issue for many cultures.

The parents expect their child to perform exceptionally well compared to others in their classroom and they put the unnecessary pressure on them, which can be very damaging for the child. This can impact their self-esteem. They live in fear and experience depression due to all the pressure of their parents' expectations. The children may develop animosity and deficiency due to the stresses imposed on them.

We need to understand that we don't own our children. They have their own personalities, likes and dislikes, strengths, and weaknesses. We cannot impose our ideas of success, career choices, or any lifestyle preferences onto them. Sometimes, our kids may not have the same goals as us. They may have their own views on how they want to live their lives. Of course, we provide support and guidance for them, but without the pressures of our high expectations. It is important to encourage our children and give them the tools to succeed in life by providing an upright value system and love in their upbringing.

Allow your children to carve their own path in life. Let them choose what's right for them. They will thrive when they feel seen and accepted rather than pressured, criticized, or judged.

And if you are someone who experienced such pressures as a child yourself, well firstly, heal yourself from any harmful side effects from your parents' expectations. And secondly, break the cycle and mindfully avoid repeating such a pattern in your own parenting.

Self-Reliant Mindset

Everything we perceive depends on our mindset. We must train ourselves to gain self-reliance and not depend on anyone for making us feel good. If they are good to you, be thankful. If they are not so good, then that is what they are capable of, and it has nothing to do with who you are or what you truly deserve. There's nothing to "fix" from your side. And there is no need to take offence either. You want to practice to consciously avoid letting in any unnecessary hurt.

Lowering our expectations of others can be challenging. Especially if you wear your heart on your sleeve, prepare to be destroyed by others unless you do some conscious inner work and learn to guard yourself emotionally. But remember, how you *feel* depends on how you *think*. Holding a high expectation is actually a *thinking habit*. And you hold such thoughts based on your paradigm, which is your set of beliefs on how things *should* be. Once your expectations are sorted, so will your emotions.

You want to build self-reliance in order to become content with yourself. Look at your life as an adventure, full of opportunities to explore without any expectations holding you back. If we learn to set our expectations free, we create more space for unexpected chances that can lead to growth rather than disappointment. A necessary shift in perspective can be a game changer!

When we expect others to understand us, approve of us, and treat us well, we lose ourselves in trying to live up to their expectations of us, which, many times, are created in our own minds. A lot of time, energy, and emotional efforts are invested in this kind of codependency, which is not accurately validated or rewarded.

You cannot depend on others to support and lift you up when needed. Yes, it can be an incredibly amazing feeling to have such people in your life who can give quality and genuine consideration to your relationship. Supporting you and cheering you on, giving you all the attention that you might crave, being there just when rightly needed, catering to your sensitivities, celebrating your successes, having faith in your dreams, providing support when challenges arise, and expressing genuine love towards you. It truly can be a blessing to have even one of those people in your life. But truthfully, for most of us, they only exist in some fairyland!

Having high expectations from people can cause some heart breaks. It can lead to self-pity, anger, resentment, enmity, and sadness. Now, I don't mean to say that there should be no expectations from your loved ones. There are certain things you simply expect from people who are close to you and those whom you choose to have around you in your inner circle. You choose them for a reason. But be careful! Even with these people, you need to set healthy boundaries and reasonable expectations. Codependency, in any relationship, can have negative consequences.

Do the right thing according to you and allow surprises. In this way, you will be able to take on a wide variety of difficult situations without losing much sleep!

Don't Seek Reciprocation

Even though, mostly, you will find people reciprocating good behaviour, don't expect it. There are many relations that you don't get to choose. If you see them less frequently, it is easier to have lower expectations of them. You can willingly be on the giving end, without strings attached! If it hurts, give space and keep things formal.

For the longest time, I had built my expectations based on how good I was towards others. But again, it was wrong of me to judge someone else's capacity to give back based on my own. Do what you genuinely can without expectations of any returns. God sees all good. Let that be enough for you! If you are content in your own life, this will come easily to you. When expectations of others are lower, you feel lesser pressure from someone else imposing their expectations on you as well.

> *Act with kindness but do not expect gratitude.*
> —Confucius

Also, when you are not expecting and when people surprise you pleasantly, you are ever so grateful. It's like a surprise gift. It's all about how you train your mind to think. Your mindset can miserably imprison you or dramatically set you free. It can make you terribly unhappy or exceptionally blissful. You choose how to feel.

When expectations from other people are minimized, you become mindful of not judging others' behaviour in relationships and that frees you. You don't seek approvals, appreciation, or reciprocation. You stop keeping score and you'll be able to meet people with a neutral/positive energy. You choose healing and joy as opposed to drama and suffering as you let go of expectations in relationships.

Reflect

1. Examine your personal life and think about ways you are holding high expectations in your life.
2. How is that effecting you?
3. Where can you lower your expectations?
4. How will that change your life?

Talk to yourself like someone you love.

—Brené Brown

Practice Self-Love

A few years back when I heard the term *self-love*, I discarded the idea completely and didn't think very positively of it. I assumed it was arrogant, needless, and self-centered. I felt like it was a luxury for those who may have too much time on their hands. How could I not feel like that? Our generation was taught this way. We learned the importance of success. We learned to work hard. We learned to take good care of our families. But we didn't learn how to keep ourselves fuelled for that journey.

Self-love is our foundation. Everything builds on top of this foundation. I later came to realize that it is the ultimate necessity for every human being. Especially because of our perfectionistic desires to reach some unrealistic standards of greatness. Otherwise, we are *not good enough*! Do you know what we mean when we think we're not good enough? We actually mean that we are not worthy of our own love, let alone others' love and acceptance. That is a big problem!

I notice that many of my clients find it very hard to love themselves. It seems to be such an unfamiliar practice for people. It may be seen as something reserved for the privileged. Where, in reality, self-love is a core feeling that everyone must develop. If we've been raised to put others first, self-love can often feel selfish or egoistic. Setting aside time for our needs often causes feelings of guilt as we struggle to give ourselves permission to experience self-love.

If you believe having a high regard for yourself is indulgent, conceited, or arrogant, you need an *inner shift*. The greater your self-love, the greater will be your love for others. The inverse is also true: hatred of others is indicative of self-loathing.

We all get too caught up, at one point in time or another, in comparing to others, people pleasing, overworking, and self-criticizing. We habitually neglect ourselves and become inadequate in building our confidence. What do we get in return? A low self-esteem, lack of achievement, unhealthy habits, and discontent with our lives. We find it harder to love others. We envy others and feel less than them. We feel burnt out and unfulfilled. We seek validation from others while giving less importance to ourselves. We expect to feel worthy of love externally without doing the inner work ourselves. We must see where we can step up and take responsibility for developing our image and value in our own minds. We are whole and worthy, and we need to embrace that.

Somehow, in most cultures, women are supposed to serve others before themselves. We are programed to sacrifice our personal needs for others in our lives, especially as mothers. Although we are slowly bringing more awareness towards this, the subconscious conditioning still triggers guilt within us for taking time out for our own well-being. This is one of the reasons why it becomes so difficult to grasp the concept of self-love for many of the women I coach.

I remember as a young mom, thinking of joining the gym, dressing up at home, or getting a massage, made me feel selfish. I was fully invested in fulfilling my role as a mother. As if I couldn't simultaneously be self-caring and care for loved ones in my life? Somewhere within my belief system, deep down, I felt unworthy of my own love and care. Perhaps I expected it from someone else externally and forgot to look for it within myself. I made excuses for myself when I didn't take care of my health. Procrastination was my middle name! I had given up way too much of myself in order to live up to some kind of standards, unaware of what it was that truly made me happy. I didn't realize I was lacking self-love. And I know this is not just my story!

To gain full benefit from this chapter, please also read the next two chapters that follow, which deal with how lack of self-love impacts you.

What Is Self-Love?

In order to fully understand this concept, it is important to know what self-love is *not*. Self-love is not a need to be better or more deserving than other people. It is not being boastful or egotistical. It is not about spending heaps of money on worldly possessions, expensive clothes, and maintaining appearances. It is not an inauthentic, fake idea of self. It is not conditional upon attaining any desired outcomes. And it's definitely not a narcissistic need of attaining importance or praise from others. Actually, egotists and narcissists don't love themselves. A "big ego" is often a compensation for lack of self-love.

What is self-love then? Self-love is a special appreciation for oneself that grows from actions that support our physical, mental, emotional, and spiritual growth. Self-love means having a high regard for your overall wellness and happiness. It means taking care of your own needs and not sacrificing your well-being to please others. It means prioritizing yourself, not settling for less than you deserve. Self-love is a pre-requisite for personal growth and mastery.

My detailed study of this topic revealed to me that self-love essentially comprises of three components: self-awareness, self-esteem, and self-care. These aspects are interconnected and need to be intentionally developed to gain a wholesome understanding.

When you bring awareness towards your thoughts and feelings, it enables you to redirect the energy you put out and receive mindfully. You take control of what you let in, the people you choose to befriend, the content you consume, and how you manage your emotions, etc. This awareness leads to treating oneself with care and building healthy habits. Honouring yourself builds self-esteem. Self-esteem has every-thing to do with being content and comfortable with who you are, where you are in life, and what you have. This takes conscious work. With a high self-worth, you don't dismiss yourself or compare yourself to others. Self-love also entails being compassionate and forgiving toward yourselves when you suffer, fail, or feel inadequate. It is first a mindset, then a practice.

Shift Your Thoughts

The sooner you realize your worthiness for deserving your own love and attention, the more favorable personal effort you'll be able to embody. Don't dismiss the idea by telling me, "I don't have time for myself right now." I have heard that especially a lot from mothers. And I have also been of those who put others first and delayed practicing self-care for a later time. Why do we feel guilt for putting ourselves first? Over time, we diminish our self-worth, which becomes harder to recover later in life.

We all use this phrase "I don't have time" so much that it has become our lazy excuse for anything we don't do. We say, "I'll lose my weight next year after my kid is older" or "I'll start my small business in a few years" or "I'll get my hair done before a wedding." Notice that we actually *plan* to do things at a later time by verbalizing it and affirming to ourselves. Such as, "I'll work out regularly in my forties" implying and believing that *I don't have time now!*

Enough excuses! You need your attention *now,* not *another time!* Because guess what? That time never comes. You only have now. You must realize how important you are. All outcomes in your life depend on your quality of self-love. Getting yourself to take serious actions requires shifting your mind to strongly believe that your progress depends on it. If you don't prioritize yourself, your life will evidently depict that.

Besides, who said self-love was only about *doing* something? Your actions always follow your thoughts. You need to first work on changing your thoughts about yourself. If you can't seem to practice good self-care, perhaps you think that you are not deserving of it. One must develop worthiness from within, firstly through beliefs about oneself, and secondly through the actions that follow. Let's shift your self-beliefs from within.

> *The real difficulty is to overcome how you think about yourself.*
> —Maya Angelou

Why Practice Self-Love?

Well firstly, because you deserve to! God created us in perfection. Just appreciating His flawless creation requires self-love and admiration. We don't love ourselves conditionally, we love ourselves first and then invest in ourselves to continuously become valuable.

> *"Indeed, We created humans in the best form."*
> —Quran, 95:4

Aside from knowing why you are lovable and loved, here are some other reasons:

- Self-love motivates you to make healthy choices in life. When you hold yourself in high esteem, you're more likely to choose things that nurture your well-being and serve you well.

- It allows you to become more aware of what you think, feel, or need. When your needs are met, you can give from a place of abundance.

- Self-love allows you to be kind, patient, gentle, and compassionate towards yourself—how you are with someone whom you care about.

- It allows you to develop yourself into becoming your best version as you bring awareness towards what kind of self-work is needed for you.

- When you honour yourself, you feel good enough, and there is no room for jealousy. You can be happy for others because you love yourself and feel fulfilled inside.

To love and care for others, your pre-requisite is self-love. Flight attendants always tell you to put your masks on before helping others with theirs. *Why?* Because you can't help others if you can't breathe. Self-love works the same way. You may have heard, "You can't pour from an empty cup." When you give from an empty place, you further drain your energy which leads to a sense of depletion and exhaustion. However, when you fill up on self-love, you'll be giving from a full tank. This type of giving feels very fulfilling.

What Does Self-Love Mean to You?

Self-love can mean something different for each person. Once we work on fully discovering the *self,* we must then grow into practicing *self-acceptance.* It allows us to fully understand the need to feed our mind, body, and soul wholeheartedly. Appreciating what we love about ourselves is the key to evolving into the person we desire to become.

For example, self-love can mean talking to and about yourself positively, prioritizing yourself, trusting yourself, having confidence in your abilities, setting healthy boundaries, and forgiving yourself when you fall short or make mistakes.

For many people, self-love is a way to practice self-care. To practice self-care, we often need to listen to our bodies. Notice how you carry yourself and see what change will bring you happiness. Take breaks from work and move/stretch or go for walks in nature. Put the phone down and connect with yourself or others or do something creative. Dress nicely. Improve the quality of your sleep. Eat healthy. Book yourself a massage and disconnect to recharge yourself.

Self-care is a key aspect of self-love as it rejuvenates us. It helps to bring about feelings of excitement, courage, and satisfaction to pursue our life goals. If we don't pay much attention to self-care, then we may feel demotivated, uninspired, and incompetent. You can't feel enthusiasm about what's next if you don't honour your present. When you become aware of the attention you need from yourself, you learn to cultivate your growth with care. In doing so, you remind yourself that you deserve to have your personal needs met.

Self-love can also mean having a better self-image. Most people have a low opinion of themselves. They don't like themselves enough to deserve any better treatment, from themselves and from others. Self-love means accepting yourself and embracing even the difficult parts of yourself. Validating everything about you with compassion. It requires a positive mindset about yourself and actions to prove that you are worthy of self-love.

Ways to Practice Self-Love

Shifting your attention towards yourself requires intentional work. Here are some ways you can love yourself:

- Recognize and prioritize your needs—physical, emotional, spiritual, or mental. Decide and plan for the practices you want to adopt and accommodate into your lifestyle.

- Become mindful of your inner voice. Be conscious of your self-talk and notice how it makes you feel. Everything originates in your mind. Your thoughts create feelings, and your feelings bring about actions accordingly. Work on eliminating any negative self-beliefs you may possess.

- Bring awareness towards your difficult feelings and understand the causes. This can allow you to introduce some deep inner work if you find it hard to love yourself. Dedicate yourself to finding solutions to overcome your difficult feelings such as anger, sadness, loneliness, jealousy, resentment, hurt, worry, etc. Journal about your feelings as you process them with care.

- Use affirmations on a regular basis. Self-love affirmations are powerful statements that can change your beliefs about yourself. Repeat in the morning or right before bed, so the words can sink into your subconscious mind. Here are some examples:
  - I am worthy of love.
  - I carry strength, courage, and resilience within me.
  - I can overcome any challenge life gives me.
  - I have an abundant life.
  - I am beautiful and am created with perfection.
  - I love and appreciate myself.
  - I am authentic and respect my limitations.

- Practice good self-care. Nourish yourself daily with healthy activities, great nutrition, exercise, proper sleep, and meaningful social interactions, etc. Make time for yourself. Cultivate some good self-loving rituals internally and externally.

Don't we all want to be loved and accepted by others? Loving others can only originate from self-love because it is an expansion of the love you have for yourself. Build a loving relationship with yourself as it sets the tone for any other relationship. Happy people's lives are products of building habits that support their relationship with themselves.

Reflect

1. How much do you love yourself on a scale from 1 to 10?
2. Write down ten things you love about yourself (attributes, practices, attitudes, etc.). This should take you no longer than one minute. If you take longer, we need to do more work!
3. What new practices can you add to enhance your self-love?

I can't tell you the key to success, but the key to failure is trying to please everyone.

—Bill Cosby

Stop People Pleasing

One of the biggest turning points on my self-awareness path was when I understood that I needed to please myself and not everyone else. Previously, I desired for others to love and accept me. I was very good-hearted in my attempts to achieve that, however, I realized that it was a self-destructive path. Not only was it tiring, but it was also a sure-fire way to lose myself in the process. I forgot to tend to my own needs and find my own purpose. In many ways, I lived more for others than for myself. It may sound like a righteous path, but, with the wrong intentions, it can strip you of your self-esteem and make you unhappy.

What is wrong with the intention to please others? you may ask. Well, the intention mostly comes from a place of insecurity, wanting to be accepted, expecting reciprocation, wanting to prove yourself, or needing to feel loved and acknowledged. An act towards others can be the same but significantly distinguished with a needy intention or a soulful one. And this intention might be hidden to others or even unknown to the people pleasers themselves, until it begins to make them feel resentful and unhappy.

People pleasing can turn into a vicious cycle of chronic stress and anxiety. If you have the constant feeling like you are too busy and doing things for everyone else except yourself, you might be stuck in this cycle. You could be in any arrangement such as a spouse, sibling, parent, friend, or co-worker and find yourself stuck in situations where you end up fulfilling requests and favours of others. People may exploit you because they don't realize that you are overextending yourself. They don't know if you don't tell them!

Who Is a People Pleaser?

A people pleaser is empathetic, nice, and always ready to help. Aren't we all that person from time to time? Yes, but this is different! People pleasers may unwillingly go along with others in hopes to make everyone happy. You can always count on them for a favour. In fact, many times, they end up doing things for other people resentfully. Most of the time, instead of being liked for this attribute, they end up getting used and abused for it while finding distortion and inauthenticity in relationships. A people pleaser rarely gets to focus on their own needs and fulfillment.

So, isn't it someone who struggles to set boundaries? Well, yes. Most people pleasers need a lot of help in that area; however, it is not as simple as just that! People pleasers may need to understand a few more distinctions about this pattern. Where setting boundaries can be necessary in practically every interaction with others, the core problem of a people pleaser may have to do with their deeper motivation behind it, as well as how much they value themselves. Some people pleasers may not realize how inauthentic they become due to the disconnect with their own needs, goals, passions, and feelings. They are unable to tune in and honour their true selves. Some of these people may actually have a few great disciplinary boundaries with themselves but struggle setting them with others.

In any relationships, when your people-pleasing pattern is stimulated, you may be attracted to people who are controlling, because they think they know what is best and are happy to lead the way. Talking to my clients, I've noticed that this dynamic can go both ways. They may initially like you because you will let them be in charge. You allow them to over-perform while you underperform. Over time, this type of a relationship can be exhausting, belittling, and unfulfilling for both parties. It can ruin a relationship because there are no clear boundaries. Unwillingly giving in can make you lose yourself. And not knowing what you stand for can confuse others.

People pleasers devote very little time to taking care of their own health and well-being. If you are a people pleaser, most of the times your heart is in the right place. You have high empathy and are looking to be accepted. Wanting to take care of others is an exceptional thing. In fact, the world needs more people with high empathy. However, if you are people pleasing at the expense of yourself and expecting reciprocation, love, or attention, you'll be hurting yourself.

> *When you say "yes" to others, make sure you aren't saying "no"*
> *to yourself.*
> —Paulo Coehlo

Why We Become People Pleasers

Two main fears may lead to this behaviour: fear of rejection, the core feeling that, If I don't make this person happy, they might leave me or stop liking me; and the fear of failure, the core feeling that, If I make a mistake, I will disappoint this person and/or be punished. This mindset gives rise to anxiety, low self-esteem, codependency, and many other problems. Our fears keep us stuck and disempower us. Therefore, any fear-led action must be questioned and dealt with.

Many of us struggle with people pleasing starting from our childhood, when we crave our parents' love and attention, wishing to please them. We do everything right, so we avoid getting in trouble. As innocent children seeking validation, perhaps with unmet emotional needs, we adopt the habit to stay on our toes, trying to "fix" something broken. In such situations, a parent typically fluctuates between idealizing and undervaluing the child, but rarely expresses genuine love for who the child really is. When a parent's love and acceptance for a child is determined by reaching set criterions, the child then copes by unconsciously shrinking their own needs and strives to put the parent's needs first, in fear of disappointing them. And then this same pattern continues into the schools and then friendships, adult relationships, and even workplaces.

There could be different motivations behind a people pleaser. Someone may develop the tendency to fake an impression on others to win them over. Yet another may strive to become a high achieving individual or *perfectionistic* to get others' approvals. And someone may be addicted to seeking attention through putting on a show, such as many unknowingly do on social media. Whatever your motivation, it is quite possible to begin shifting your behaviour by doing some necessary inner work.

In order to bring the change in such behaviour, one needs to become aware of the underlining motives of people pleasing and understand how they may have picked up the habit. After gaining awareness, one may need to change some thinking patterns and work on developing themselves to grow their self-esteem. Gaining a higher regard for oneself can boost one's self worth, thereby, reducing the need to seek validation and acceptance from others. Refer to the chapter on Self-love.

Are You a People Pleaser?

Read over these statements to see if they apply to you under any circumstances:

- I try to be who someone wants me to be.
- It is hard for me to know what I want.
- I avoid speaking my mind and expressing my feelings.
- I find it easier to go along with others' wishes or opinions.
- It is difficult for me to say no to others.
- It is hard for me to take initiative and do new things.
- I don't feel worthy enough to set my dream goals.
- I try to be nice rather than expressing how I *really* feel.
- I avoid conflicts and confrontations with others.
- I want everyone to like and accept me.

If you seem to agree with a few of the above, you are a people pleaser to a degree. What essentially happens when you are people pleasing is that, overtime, you lose your authenticity and tend to wear a mask in social situations. If someone says something that you disagree with, you find it hard to share your opinion. You put others first and forget about your own needs. In doing so, you forget what you wish to achieve or even hesitate to set goals. You become distant from your own intuitive callings. You are influenced easily. And you are that *pleasing* person while feeling miserable and *unpleasant* inside.

Think of a situation when you rushed to fulfill others' demands without even considering whether the demands were reasonable. Shouldn't we be able to say *no* when we need to? Isn't that more authentic? Why do you feel the need to fulfill high demands and expectations? It sends others the wrong messages. And to be honest, in my experience, most people are never "pleased" no matter how much you lose yourself over them. So not only do you lose authenticity and create confusion, but you also lose your motivation. Internally, there is a huge conflict within, that needs to be resolved and only you have the power to create the *inner shift*.

Overcoming People Pleasing

You want to be kind and helpful when you can extend yourself *willingly*. When your own needs are met and you are coming from a place of *wanting* to give, the impact of your favours is much greater than when you unwillingly force yourself to just be "nice." You want to practice giving from a loving, deliberate place without feeling less than anyone or under any sort of pressure. When we are self-assured, we extend ourselves willfully. We don't seek approvals when we already feel confident within ourselves.

How healthy is your self-esteem? People struggle with asserting themselves when they are unhappy with how they feel about themselves. We all have our higher selves hidden inside of us, waiting to be discovered. Sometimes, as an act of self-love, we need to heal parts of us that may have been damaged overtime. Seeking therapy/coaching to sort out some inner turmoil can surely bring forth a version of yourself that you can truly admire and own. The shift must begin from the *inside-out*.

When you find the courage within to assert yourself, begin some external work. Look for the places where there is immediate room for setting some limits with your family, friends, coworkers, etc. It comes down to what is an considered an unrealistic expectation, a demand, or a request/favour. You get to define your limits. When asked a favour, check: Do I have time? Am I available? Am I neglecting myself/family in some important way, etc.? Am I willing? Learn about setting boundaries in the next chapter.

The idea of asserting yourself also goes for your values. If you are sure of who you are and you respect your values and viewpoints, you will express them unapologetically. Authenticity is admirable and appealing. People will respect and honour your values more when you are authentic. You won't need to go out of your way to gain praise and acceptance. Real relationships are built when you can be yourself, share your ideas, and be flexible without any fear of judgement. Otherwise, you compromise your values and feel unhappy and unworthy in struggles to maintain some sort of a false image. When you share your truth, you also hear others respectfully and acknowledge your differences rather than impose upon one another.

You are someone valuable and you have wisdom of your own. When you are with the right person, communicating your needs will be easy. This takes some pressure off them as they understand you better and you will feel seen. Not knowing what is or is not okay with you can be detrimental to any relationship. Here are some helpful points:

- Be good, giving, and kind. But don't do it for the wrong reasons. Expecting others to like and validate you for your efforts, will only tire you and harm you.
- Don't neglect your priorities. You are the main character of your story. Give yourself special attention.
- Know your values to protect yourself from being misunderstood. Don't worry too much about others' judgements.
- Set boundaries and communicate them clearly. (Refer to the next chapter)
- Explore your willingness to give. You can't pour from an empty cup. Be sure to give from an abundant place inside.
- Practice assertiveness. Stick to your decisions, values, and opinions unapologetically. People will admire you for that.

You need to be able to grow and flourish as a person and that requires freedom from people pleasing. You will lift the heavy weight of needing to convince others to like you and approve of you. Your focus will shift on feeding your mind and soul. Others will respect and admire you even more because self-confidence is very attractive.

> *Because one believes in oneself, one doesn't try to convince others. Because one is content with oneself, one doesn't need others' approval. Because one accepts oneself, the world accepts him or her.*
>
> —Lao Tzu

Reflect

1. Think of ways you practice people pleasing and how it affects you negatively.
2. What do you need to change in your behaviour?
3. Who will you ask for help?
4. What are some practical ways you can grow your self-esteem? List some action steps for yourself.

Guard you heart, mind, and time. Those three things will determine the health of everything else in your life.

—Andrena Sawyer

Set Healthy Boundaries

Listen! If you want to pursue a life where you aim to be content and successful in your personal and social goals, you will need to create some space. A space where you feel safe, peaceful, and free. It will allow you to function in *creative mode*, which is more in synch with your inner self. The more distractions and external noise you let in, the more it could dilute your purpose. We must look at how much control external factors have on our lives and how that impacts us internally. In today's world especially, there is too much noise outside of your sacred space, that pushes you farther away from your inner calling. You must guard this space and grow from inside-out. This is where setting boundaries plays an important role.

One gets to decide on what terms they give from their time, energy, and capacity. You willfully give from your mental, emotional, physical space. No one gets to demand it from you if it taxes you in anyway. Now this can be confusing to understand as we all sacrifice ourselves in various ways to give to others. Such as a mother scarifies for her little ones. The key is knowing if such a sacrifice is made by choice or unwillingly. Life requires many sacrifices, but you must choose them. You can be selfless towards caring for your loved ones and you can certainly give with a big heart. Setting boundaries is not about that! It is about how you deal with yourself and others on a regular basis. To further understand, please answer a few questions for yourself:

- Do you feel obligated to answer your texts or calls at unsuitable times?

- Do you keep agreeing to do things that you really don't want to do?
- Do you tolerate disrespect to avoid conflict or confrontation?
- Do you feel overworked, overcommitted, and tired?
- Do you feel like you have no time for yourself, leading you to feel resentful, angry, and unhappy?
- Do you feel manipulated, pressured, controlled, or helpless?
- Do you feel lack of confidence and inability to assert yourself?

Well, if you said "yes" to a few of the above, you need to set some boundaries! Many people fail to establish necessary boundaries and have them known to others. Some people find this to be easy, as it may come naturally to them. For many of us though, setting boundaries feels uncomfortable. We feel guilty and anxious when we are required to assert our needs. Going along with the flow, or just saying "yes" seems easier at times. But when it becomes a habit, you might feel like a door mat as others will take advantage of you or mistreat you.

Without setting boundaries, you might become a *people pleaser* and end up neglecting your own needs. You may fear being rejected, so you allow others to decide things for you, giving them control over you. You may feel frustrated because you are frequently in codependent relationships that lack a balanced exchange of give and take. You are unable to connect with yourself, feeling lost or confused about your values, goals or opinions. It can make you develop a passive attitude about your life, which disempowers you. At its worse, not setting boundaries allows others to manipulate or abuse you. All the above can negatively impact your self-esteem, which can be deeply depressing.

Over time, I have realized that having personal boundaries is the secret to maintaining balance and peace, even if it causes for me to be misunderstood at times. I made unfamiliar choices which required some boundaries, especially as a homeschooling parent. For example, I had to make myself unavailable for people at certain timings to be able to dedicate my time towards my kids. I also learned how to answer back when people directed any negativity towards my choices, blocking out any attacks or opposing presumptions. Aside from that, I practiced setting healthy boundaries with my children for us to thrive in a homeschooling environment. Knowing what we allow and what our limits are, can feel very peaceful.

Benefits of Setting Boundaries

Personal boundaries are a great way to take care of yourselves. Here are some ways setting boundaries can be of benefit to you:

- They help create and maintain a healthy self-image and elevate your self-respect.
- They allow a safe space where personal development and mindfulness can grow.
- They help manage demands on your time and emotions.
- They protect your right to making choices, which empowers you.
- They allow more mental, emotional, and physical energy.
- They provide the freedom to express your needs and expectations.
- They allow you to let others know what to expect from you and how you want to be treated. This transforms your relationships.
- They improve our self-awareness and confidence as we allow our values to be known.
- They help reduce stress and improve the quality of your life.

Nice or Kind?

People think they are simply being "nice" when they go with the flow and allow others to dominate them. Ask yourself, how does it actually feel to be the nice one? I remember trying hard to please others. I thought being nice was a likeable trait. Being there for others and fulfilling their demands felt like the right thing to do. I tried my hardest to be on their good side. I just genuinely wanted a peaceful relationship with everyone.

I admired that trait of mine for the longest time until I began to notice how it made me feel inside.

Was I pleasing everyone else at the cost of losing my own happiness and peace of mind? Was anybody really seeing my efforts to please them as much as I thought? Were my efforts being reciprocated as I expected? Or was I being used and forgotten? All of this was leading to resentment, sadness, and hurt.

I realized that my "niceness" was not coming from a compassionate and kind place. It was rather my need to get something in return. Some sort of goodness in exchange that would make me happy. Acceptance? Appreciation? Approval? Perhaps in doing so I had given the power of my happiness to others. It was a forced behaviour that was somewhat manipulative without me realizing how it harmed me in the end. What was I missing? Boundaries!

And believe me, each one of you has experienced this cycle in one way or another and the feelings associated with it. Some are in miserable relationships due to this, and others are failing at parenting or suffering at work. It takes a lot of self-awareness to see how your social behaviours affect your own well-being.

Many people would argue, Well I can't hurt others, or, I only try to be nice! I want to mention a key difference between *being nice* and *being kind*. When you are nice, you are looking for approval and acceptance by saying "yes" to others. When you are kind, however, you are simply giving with no intention of expecting reciprocation in return. You are fulfilled when you say "yes" *by choice*. There is no need to prove to anyone anything once you are self-assured and secure in your position or authority. You give generously to fulfill yourself and on your terms. What you seek may be a reward beyond this world. It could be a deep spiritual feeling. Or simply a way to practice self-compassion.

> *Compassionate people ask for what they need. They say "no" when they need to, and when they say yes, they mean it. They're compassionate because their boundaries keep them out of resentment.*
>
> —Brené Brown, *Rising Strong*

The Art of Saying "No"

A big part of setting boundaries is knowing what to say "yes" to and when to say "no." Most people struggle with that. Especially in a time where we are bombarded with unnecessary exposure to external stimuli that can interfere with our inner peace. Saying "no" is your superpower! Know your values, positions, and reasons. Bring awareness to everything that impact your decision making. Be firm on your ways so others can't persuade you against your will. No brainwashing. No guilt trips. No manipulating. You are the captain of your ship!

This may include saying "no" to things that are not okay with you, such as disallowing others to go through your personal belongings, take their anger out on you unjustly, humiliate you, impose their opinion on you, invade your mental or emotional space, or demand your time when you are not available, etc. By doing so, you are setting boundaries as you say "no" to others while saying "yes" to you. Give yourself the permission to say "no" to anything that is not aligned with you or drains your energy. Authenticity is important. If you say "yes" to others resentfully, you might as well say "no" authentically and be at peace with yourself.

Saying "yes" to you comes after saying "no" to unnecessary things in your life. Cutting out things that suck up your energy is also a way to setting personal boundaries. Once the unnecessary things (bad habits, addictions, unwilling commitments) that take up too much time are sorted and dealt with, you carve out more time for productivity. This will allow time for doing things you enjoy such as a passion project, working out, listening to podcasts, reading a book, writing, volunteering, connecting with like-minded people, growing spirituality, exploring nature, or practicing a hobby. This will assure you that it is you who manages your time and not others.

Learning how to say "no" to others is an art one must learn. If not said right, it can often create misunderstandings. But agreeing to do something or allowing things to happen that don't work for you, can be difficult. Knowing how to say "no" politely is an important part of asserting yourself and setting boundaries so people may respect your decision and understand your reasoning. Be kind, yet firm.

A dear client of mine once reached out to me all frazzled. She couldn't say "no" to a friend's birthday party that she had no interest or energy to attend. Her kids were sick at home, and she now needed to change her plan. She just felt bad for telling her friend that she must cancel. She was adamant that she must go and there's no way to say "no" or else, she'll be upset. As much as she knew that going to the party was not suitable for her and she needed to attend to her own priorities, she found it extremely difficult to say "no." We worked on her internal block and challenged her to say "no" without feeling any guilt. She struggled to say her truth but took the challenge. To her surprize, her friend understood completely and had no issues at all. So, this whole resistance was self-built within her based on her assumptions and was only real in her own mind until she decided to breakthrough it.

It is important to be straightforward. Instead of saying "maybe" or "I don't think so," be unambiguous in your answer. For example, "Sorry, I have already committed to something else. I hope you understand," or, "I'm honoured that you asked me, but my plate is quite full for now."

Give a brief explanation of why you are saying no. This can help soften your answer and help the person understand why you declined. Keep it short and sweet. It's not necessary to give lengthy explanations. Keep it simple and courteous, such as, "I would love to join you, but I'm feeling a little overwhelmed with work right now." When you set these clear boundaries, people learn to respect your needs and you feel at peace.

Where to Set Boundaries

Begin by setting some boundaries in your personal lifestyle. The more self-disciplined you become, the easier you set boundaries with others. A very relevant place to set strong boundaries is with using devices and social media. If we allow ourselves to attend to every notification all day long, we might go crazy! And the sad thing is, a lot of us are actually on our devices for many hours in a day unaware of the addiction. We must set our limits on cell phone and social media usage. Decide when and how long you will access your device for and be strict on setting your boundary. There are so many ways to explore settings and protect your choices on social media. Use the *block* tool and delete unnecessary connections online without any guilt. You decide what you allow into your life ever so mindfully.

Protect your time and energy by setting boundaries with yourself. This requires self-control. Take your time to return calls or emails. There is no urgency with most messages. Bow out of option activities if it's draining for you. Listen to yourself and honour your feelings about things. This will free up time for things you really want to pursue.

Most people who struggle with setting boundaries also struggle with negative self-talk and lack *internal boundaries*. Notice your self-talk and learn to manage it. Replace it with some positivity instead. No name-calling for yourself such as, I'm so dumb, how could I not get this? or, Why would anyone listen to me? That is detrimental to your mental health and damages your self-esteem. Another internal boundary is to quit making excuses for yourself. Such as saying, "I can't exercise because I have no time." Think of all the things you could possibly do if you didn't keep making excuses for yourself. Of course, there may be underlining issues that can be dealt with on a deeper level, but awareness is always needed for any level of transformation. Setting internal boundaries requires consistent work and self-discipline.

As you initiate setting boundaries with others, begin by mindfully guarding your exposure, as it influences you. Bring the right people into your life who respect and inspire you. Associate with positive and supportive people. Protect yourself from the naysayers and energy suckers. The complaining, rude, or gossipy types need to go. Be sure to evaluate your boundaries in your social interactions and friendships.

When faced with resistance, know that there will be haters and complainers and off-putting feedback and judgements from those who don't respect your boundaries. Those are the people you need your boundaries for in the first place, so don't be intimidated by their reactions.

Boundaries are the backbone for maintaining healthy relationships. Many relationships are suffering due to lack of boundaries. You need boundaries with your family at home, friends, relatives, and others.

It is important to also set boundaries in professional arrangements. Whether you own a business or work in a corporate environment, you need to have your own back! I developed this skill more vividly through running my small business on my terms. This included setting my working hours, choosing who I wanted to work with, fixing the cost for my services, and things I don't compromise on for my working arrangements, etc.

Same works for your corporate settings because no one knows what your needs are other than you and only you can assert them clearly. Don't allow anyone to demand work from you after work hours if that takes a toll on your life. Don't let any unnecessary pressures or corporate politics to overpower you. Design and honour your work-life balance and make it a priority.

Boundaries with Your Spouse

You might think, What do I need boundaries for with my spouse? This is a relationship where you really need to set some healthy boundaries. A boundary in a marriage is the limit of what a person is willing to accept from their spouse. Boundaries serve as a means of feeling respected, loved, and safety with one's spouse. Married couples can establish boundaries in areas, such as:

- With in-laws and family (e.g., personal details about the marriage, visiting rules, or keeping contact).
- With personal privacy (e.g., agreeing not to go through each other's phones).
- Finances and spending choices.
- How to communicate (e.g., no name calling or shouting).
- Having autonomy (i.e., the freedom to work towards goals and make decisions).
- With parenting expectations and household chores.
- Creating personal space and respect.
- Rules of sharing things.

Of course, understanding what a boundary looks like is just one part of the puzzle. The next step is figuring out how to set a boundary effectively. Be sure to communicate your values and needs early on in your relationship and allow room to revisit things as you grow together.

To give an easy everyday example, perhaps the husband drives too recklessly, and the wife feels uneasy. She can say, "Please don't speed when I'm a passenger in our car. It makes me feel unsafe and upsets me." If your spouse wants to have a discussion you feel too exhausted to engage in, you can say, "I would love to talk about this with you but I'm really tired and not in the right headspace to discuss this tonight. Can we please make time for this tomorrow? I really need to hit the bed!" And make sure you attend to them the next day! This lets them know that you are willing to discuss things and hear them out, but you can choose to make yourself available. Sharing the same space can bring its many challenges. If your husband is a morning person and you happen to be a night owl, you may set boundaries to respect each other's needs.

Now you won't be perfect at this skill always. Both of you will make mistakes so be sure to take responsibility when you make a mistake, offer genuine apologies, and always circle back to clear, respectful communication and discussion on where improvements can be made. The more you learn to communicate well, the better boundaries you'll set and respect.

Boundaries with Your Children

I truly believe, parenting is something that should be taught before we take on the role as parents. Most of us just plunge into the unknown territory and take things as they come with its challenging surprises. With that said, know that we all need some clear boundaries with a parent-child relationship to create harmony within a household. If the balance is off and there's tension in this regard, the parent is usually to blame. Children simply don't know what your boundaries are. This doesn't necessarily mean that you become a very strict parent. In some cultures, parents have this overpoweringly intimidating presence in the relationship. I don't support that at all, and I believe it can be traumatizing for children.

Certain respectful cultural values in this dynamic are admirable, as long as a pleasant, loving relationship is established. There are some clear lines that shouldn't be crossed by your children, and you have to make it very clear to them. Precisely define your boundaries and try to stick to your principles rather than randomly reacting to your emotions.

State your boundaries directly and with matching body language, like you mean it, yet with love. Such as, "Sweetheart, please always knock on the door before you come in our bedroom." You might have to repeat and be consistent. Also, recognize when they have stuck by the boundaries you've set. Praise them and acknowledge their efforts. Children love to be noticed for something they did, especially when it's from their parents. This makes them feel loved and cherished. It motivates them to stick to these boundaries in future. Positive reinforcement is great at maintaining a child's good behaviour.

You can set a boundary if you need to train your children to learn to respect your time. For example, your child wants to play a game with you at a time you are busy. You can let them know, "I'm not available right now, (insert your reason) but I would love to play with you in an hour." This way you allow space for yourself and provide an expected time for your child, so they learn to respect your time. It will prevent the burn out from always saying "yes" to your family's needs.

Now even with all the boundaries communicated with your child, you might still struggle implementing them and they might struggle to always respect and honour your boundary. Always have expectations according to their developmental stages. Your parenting is much easier if your children know what is expected of them. You decide how you reasonably hold them accountable for crossing a boundary. If you set the tone for your relationship early on in your parenting, you'll notice certain things will become second nature to them. A lot of manners are taught through setting examples for them, such as always knocking the door before entering the bedrooms, asking for permission before sharing each other's belongings, respecting personal space, or not interrupting during conversations, etc.

Many times, it requires for you to practice what you preach. Respect your spouse's boundaries and also your child's. Yes! Your child also has boundaries. Sometimes we over-function for our kids. We helicopter-parent them by jumping in and taking control instead of letting our child work things out for him/herself. You must allow personal space, freedom to choose certain things, take their time to finish something, or make career choices, etc. These things look different according to their age. They need more privacy as they grow older, and you need to respect that as a parent.

How to Set Boundaries

Setting boundaries is a way of honouring yourself, therefore, you must begin with some inner work. I do a lot of coaching on this subject matter, so here are a few things to think about when setting some boundaries with anyone:

- Begin with becoming more self-aware of where and why you need to set healthy boundaries.
- Identify and gain clarity regarding what is and is not acceptable to you in your life and why. Honour your values.
- Set simple and firm boundaries with a neutral tone.
- Don't expect others to know your boundaries. They can't read your mind. Explicitly communicate what you need or what works for you. There is no need to defend, debate, or overexplain yourself.
- *Ask* for what you need. It is okay to ask for things like more privacy, help around the house, peace and quiet, more time before deciding, more information before making a purchase, etc.
- Back up your boundary with action. If you give in, you invite people to ignore your needs. Your personal boundaries are based on your values and might be totally different from someone else's. So don't feel guilty about politely asserting yourself.

Reflect

1. What do boundaries look like in your life currently?

2. Where do you need to set some clear boundaries?

3. What are some ideas for how you will communicate your boundaries with others?

Life is simple, get out of your head and into the moment.

—Sylvester McNutt

Let Go

At any time, we are living in our past, present, or future. Based on our patterns and state of minds, we choose one over the other for the most times. If we're obsessed with our past, we might deal with a lot of guilt, shame, or regret due to overanalyzing, which in turn causes sadness. If we tend to be focused on our future, we might feel worried, fearful, or anxious due to overthinking what could happen. Or even indulge in a lot of planning and stressing. We do this unaware, on autopilot mode, because that is how society programs us.

Ideally, we want to live in our present, only visiting the past for reference and learnings that prepare us for our future lives. This requires for us to let go of the self-sabotaging thoughts pertaining to our pasts or futures. Living in the present promotes joy of existing through gratitude and acceptance while actively pursuing our goals with clarity. It also promotes inner peace.

Healing from the Past

Most people make their lives difficult by residing in their heads. Life happens. Things go wrong in our lives. And many unknowns do exist in our futures. We all are meant to experience imperfections, failures, mishaps, and resentments. Our past is not meant to haunt us and make us regretful.

Whatever happens to us in life is our journey to own, process, learn from, and move on from. We can extract wisdoms and life lessons, and experience growth from our past happenings. What is important to understand is that holding on is just as hard as it is to let go, however, letting go is relieving and freeing, whereas, holding on keeps you captive to your past.

Things that happened the way they did, good or bad, were meant to happen. Believe that your past was just right at that moment. Many things that happened were wrong based on what you know now, but they were right while they were happening to help you in some way. It may be hard to accept major losses, trauma, and abuse, however, there is an appropriate way to deal with and move on from any difficult life situation once you decide to let go. *Letting go* in such situations can mean that you need to allow healing. Don't underestimate your ability to heal and carry on from past happenings, no matter how wounded you felt. Humans can be very resilient and capable.

Most of us need to make the strong decision to let go and embrace our personal journey as we bravely march forward. Think, *If it served me in any way, it was good for me*. This belief about your past will help you process and heal through things easily.

Free yourself from emotional pain and toxic thoughts regarding your past. Holding on to past pain doesn't heal you. Replaying the hurtful memories repeatedly won't change anything as it would only make your wounds deeper. And regretting, wishing things were different doesn't fix anything as you can never return to your past. One needs to allow processing of unsettling events or situations and work on eventually letting go. This work may involve seeking professional support such as therapy or coaching. Allow yourself to ask for help.

Why We Hold On

We all experience pain and hurt in various ways. Our psychological reasoning behind it is to be validated and understood. Isn't that the minimal expectation at least? No! Holding on to a grudge or resentment is like injecting poison into your body repeatedly. This poison damages you inside. It serves no purpose. You might think, Well my pain is unforgivable, or, I have been through so much, how can I let go of all that I have endured? or, It's not easy to just let it all go. No one knows how I feel, and so on. Such self-talk and restrictive beliefs are not going to get people to sympathize with you or make you a bigger victim than you already might feel to be. Also, the mentality of wanting others to validate your pain doesn't serve you. Neither does masking it all and pretending that everything is fine. You must heal from your pain by understanding it, giving it meaning, making peace with it, and mindfully carry on.

We cling to unwanted stress as we hold on to our past pain. It only builds more resentment, shame, regret, and keeps us stagnant in our relationships and life. As if this act of fixation gives us power. Ironically, it does quite the opposite. Our mental clutter can end up giving us serious health problems. The feeling of wanting to have everyone understand and validate our pain before we decide to let go is a ridiculous expectation. A person who hasn't experienced your pain can't understand it. And even if they did, there is not much you get out of it for yourself. Don't expect to be validated or wait for closures. It's just not worth it. The sooner you learn this, the easier your life becomes.

Many times, we struggle with letting go because we either find it hard to accept or understand. We may get the recurring thought, Why me? or, It's unfair! We think that if we are good, we deserve good. Although it may sound fair, life simply doesn't work that way. All kinds of things will happen to you in life. Some will be good and others, not so good. When we are unexpectedly hit with something difficult, we ask ourselves, What did I do to deserve this? Well, let me ask you this: who said we deserve everything we get? How much of your life experience has been chosen by you? We don't even start off by choice. We don't even get to choose which set of parents we get, let alone where we live, who we meet, what happens accidentally, and so much more. What we get to choose is our interpretation and our response.

Some people have trouble letting go of their pain or hurtful emotions, because they think those feelings are part of their identity. I see this a lot with many of my clients. At times, they may not know who they are without their emotional pain. This makes it impossible for them to let go. Deciding to hold on to the past will hold you back from creating a strong sense of self, one that isn't defined by your past but rather by who *you want to be*. Your experience is simply an opportunity and an invitation towards growth. You decide *who* you become in the *process* of letting go. It may sound odd but painful feelings can be comfortable for you, especially if they're all you know. Discover your potential to heal. Understand and make this a healing mantra for yourself: *I am not what happens to me, I can be who I want to be.*

Here's a truth bomb for you! We don't get awareness, wisdom, strength, or life lessons through ease or comfort. That is simply the bitter reality of levelling up and becoming a better version of yourself. You will have to let go of the idea of understanding the reasons for what happens as a *victim* of life events and evolve into the *victor*.

You don't get to choose a lot of the things in life. You do have a choice regarding the kind of attitude you wish to take along. With the correct attitude, you can be happy and thrive in any situation.

Personal Story

There was a time when I felt the need to understand everything in life. I did pretty well with that most of the times, however, I had to shed that need and simply learn to go with the flow of life with an upgraded attitude. Just when I had worked on letting go of some negative past experiences and forgave many things about my life—I thought I had reached the point where I could be in control of most things—I was tested with new surprises in my life. These new tests required a newer version of me that I had to grow into.

As much as not being a victim of your situations is important, some things will happen in your life that you will never expect or know how to process. That is where you let go of the need to control the *divine plan*. The One that controls the turning of days and nights and changing of the seasons has a plan for you as well. If you are spiritual, this will make a lot of sense. There is so much out of our hands, and we must learn to flow with acceptance and grace. Distinguishing what is in our control and what's not is vital. Our thoughts and actions are certainly in our control.

It was my daughter's diagnosis of type 1 diabetes that really changed the expectation to know why we go through the things that we do and simply trusting the divine plan. Instead of thinking, Why me? I was compelled to think, Why not me? I began to practice acceptance through a new understanding: I don't have to understand why this happened. I needed to reframe this traumatizing life event for our family as something God specifically chose us for, to bring much strength, awareness, and purpose into our lives!

Alongside mourning an extreme irreversible health condition and the overwhelming sadness, I also began to feel honoured for this difficult test. It is certainly not for the fainthearted! My heart aches for my daughter, but along with her, I think of many other kids in the world who don't have the needed care for this condition. The new level of gratitude that I feel is a profound spiritual expansion of my old self. I have a new appreciation for this life's blessings that most take for granted. I grew in new ways through this tragedy. I get to practice reframing our daily challenges positively. I do wish this reality could change, and I will never stop praying for that, but in the meantime, I need to be mindful of my blessings and everything that I do have control over. I truly have let go of any control or worries associated with my daughter's chronic life condition, as it continuous to impact our lives as a family in a way I never imagined. I choose to gracefully accept with courage as I see my brave girl battle it every day with a sweet smile on her face.

Worry pretends to be necessary but serves no useful purpose.
—Eckhart Tolle

How to Let Go

Make the decision to let go of anything that keeps you stuck in the past as well as any worries about the future. Don't obsess about planning extensively for the future while forgetting to rejoice in the present. Recognize that you are constantly evolving into a better version of yourself. Therefore, difficult setbacks from the past don't reside in your mind or in your heart. You take whatever you've got and are dedicated to transform and create what's yet to come. Where you are right now is perfect in relation to where you have been. In other words, your past was perfect in order for you to become the person you are now. This mindset truly heals you from your past and also helps overcome your limitations.

Through *self-love* comes the desire for self-healing and seeking highest good for oneself. Not because you are not good enough or need fixing. But because you love and accept yourself and understand your limitless potential and what you truly deserve.

If you find it hard to let go of the past or are consumed by worries of the future, here are some tips that could help:

- Make sincere intentions to let go and aim to grow through the process.

- Create a list of all the reasons you need to let go. How will letting go impact your life positively? Reflect on this deeply.

- Don't waste your time and energy trying to convince others to validate you. You can't rely on someone else to give you closure or heal your wounds.

- Question your need to hold on to your hurt or worries. You will begin to let go when you find that the stress to hold on does not serve you in any way.

- Feel and release emotions. If you tend to mask it and let the bitterness build inside, you must learn to feel emotions, process them, and move on. If you share with someone who can hold space for you, you'll have a release, and you would no longer bottle up your emotions. But remember, the intention is not to complain or gain sympathy, rather to heal and let go.

- Journal about what's troubling for you. Journaling helps to reflect on things as you spend some time getting things out of your system.

- Learn to forgive. Resentment and unwillingness to forgive will keep you locked in the past and prevent you from moving forward with your life. Remember, when you forgive, you aren't accepting what happened to you or pardoning another person for their offence. You're making peace with it for your own good. More on this topic in the following chapter.

- Going forward, develop the attitude to surrender to the unexpected reality of how things play out. Don't be overly invested in the outcomes and allow surprises to unfold. It will make you flexible and you'll be able to overcome things and flow with ease.

- Visualize your future. Realize that many of the things you're holding on to don't really matter in the grand scheme of things. Understand that letting your past take up too much of your present is a great loss for you. Time is your limited asset. Imagine what really matters for your future and put your energy towards building a better tomorrow based on the lessons learned today.

Your attitude determines all the outcomes in life. Being able to let go requires a strong sense of self, which gives you the ability to learn and grow from your experiences. Some ways to discover profound insights that will help you to access deep levels of contentment can be exploring shadow work, inner-child work, and going for therapy to overcome some limitations pertaining to yourself.

Reflect

1. Make a list of difficult things from your past or worries about future that you struggle to let go of.

2. How do these things impact you currently?

3. Write down some action steps for yourself to take in order to let go.

The weak can never forgive.
Forgiveness is the attribute of
the strong.

—Mahatma Gandhi

Forgive

Forgiveness is known to be a highly encouraged act. It is recommended by most religions and is considered a praiseworthy practice. However, many of us don't truly understand what it entails. How many of us genuinely forgive? What is forgiveness? Why we need to understand and practice it? What are the benefits of forgiving? And how do we truly forgive? Let's discuss.

Forgiveness is a key element of our healing process. Most people can't heal themselves because they don't know what it means to forgive. In fact, they don't intend to forgive either. The norm tends to be holding on to grudges and acting upon resulting feelings. We all know how sad that feels. The only way to overcome our negative feelings related to unfavourable happenings, is to learn to genuinely forgive.

In order to exercise our practice of forgiveness, we must know what it demands. What does forgiveness mean? Is it just an intense emotion? Or a deceptive coping mechanism? Or is it pretending to forget and accept? Is it a practice of the spiritual and pious folks alone? Or a tactic for the heart to overcome anger? Is it our intense desire to seek that closure? All of the above and more? Perhaps not such a complicated concept that we must understand properly.

I love how Oprah says, "forgiveness is giving up the hope that the past could be any different." I just love that definition! Most people might confuse forgiveness with acceptance. Understand that forgiveness is not accepting that it was okay what happened to you. Instead, accept the fact that it *has* happened to you and now you must do something about it. It is not being happy with your past always, rather choosing your future to be peaceful and wiser. So, in essence, in making the intention to forgive, you decide what you wish to choose for *yourself*. Forgiveness is an understanding that we don't expect apologies, closures, or rectification, rather *peace*.

Whether it is something relational that you must forgive or situational, the act of forgiving becomes a gift to yourself as you gradually cultivate it. This takes patience, practice, and persistence, but I assure you that forgiveness can create deep inner peace.

Why Is Forgiving Difficult?

Your common belief on this idea may be the problem! You may think that forgiveness benefits the other person and causes one to remain in loss. You may believe that forgiving is an act done towards the other. That is completely untrue! Forgiveness doesn't mean one has to rebuild a relationship or work towards reconciliation. One can very well forgive and do it solely for their own personal benefit without even letting the other person know that they are forgiven.

As well, you may find things hard to forgive because they were unfair. Or perhaps you feel those that hurt you don't deserve forgiveness. Your thirst for revenge could consume you. Maybe your ego gets in the way, and you keep justifying your truth of the matter. Perhaps you are hoping to receive an apology in the way you feel you deserve it before you forgive and get proper closure. You feel entitled to this apology. You hope the intentions behind your resistance and rebellion must be understood and addressed. These are some of the things my clients express when they feel emotionally imprisoned due to unsettled matters of the past. They need to make the *inner shift* to understand and practice forgiveness.

Your reasons to not want to forgive are based on a story in your mind. Sadly, this story is all perceived and created by *you* and is only true for you. Others see and justify things a different way than you do based on their current paradigm and understanding. Whether you agree with their perception or not, is not relevant. Who said being understood was our highest value? Well, if it happens to be yours, then please change that *now*. If you find it hard to forgive, you are the one who remains enslaved to all the feelings as a result of giving this event a home within you.

Why Forgive?

Holding on to anger, resentment, and hurt does not redeem what others have done. It only leaves you with tense muscles, a heavy heart, headache, mental strain, sadness, and even an overall dejected demeanour. The resulting feelings and actions have many dangerous ripple effects for years to follow. Anyone with common sense knows that we don't want those things for ourselves, but still, most people don't practice forgiveness.

Here's the beauty of this practice: whether you forgive yourself, others, or they forgive you, you benefit from all three situations. Forgiveness gives you happiness and lightness in life. It heals you from your past pains and brings you peace and freedom as you transform yourself for the better. It is a way to practice good emotional self-care.

We are designed to grow and if we can't forgive, we become stuck. And the longer we remain there, the more healing we need. And frankly, we don't have the time to waste while missing out on the pleasures of this life due to our inability to let go.

We forgive for our own peace of mind and ease in the heart. To relieve ourselves of the pain of resentment and anger. Let's be real, wishing for something to be erased or regretting it too much won't ever help you. And believe me, closures can feel great at times, but they could be overrated. It may sound difficult but, don't wait around for them. You will only harm yourself in doing so. Really check your expectations and see if they truly make sense.

> *Forgiveness does not change the past, but it does enlarge the future.*
> —Paul Boss

When we forgive, we free ourselves of having enmity, regret, guilt, shame, anger, and negativity—essentially everything that causes sadness and depression. Whatever is within us, takes up space in our mind, body, and soul. You want to dump out any burden you carry from holding on to the grudge and make space for new refreshing things for yourself. Forgiveness can clean out any such things that hold you back from achieving more meaningful and exciting things in life.

An Empowering Perspective Shift

I remember struggling with forgiveness when I was younger. I wanted to forgive so I could be the bigger person. But I expected the other person would at least notice and reciprocate by also changing their behaviour towards me. I was expecting good in return. It can be such a challenging thing to forgive when you are young. If only wisdom came to us without trials and hurt!

Back in my *people pleasing* days, I expected that it would be as easy as just opening up the difficult incidents and discussing what happened ever so harmoniously, thereby, understanding each other's point of views and feelings at the moment, clarifying everything nicely, and mutually agreeing to forgive and become best friends again!

Oh! The expectations! The problem with that naïve supposition was that, people don't grow at the same rate and are not as open to reflecting over past events the same way you might be. Coming to understanding myself and my inclinations as opposed to others made a huge difference for me. People cannot read our minds and we must not expect they have similar intentions as ours either. Even when we all have good intentions overall, we go about acting differently and are mostly misunderstood. I had to learn to live with being misunderstood while protecting my good heartedness. As I grew wiser, I also had to learn how to forgive myself for my naivety to overcome any related hurt.

My journey of self-discovery has allowed me to re-evaluate what forgiveness means for me and, most importantly, it taught me that an apology is not required in order to be freed. It has opened a whole new perspective in my life, one where I put my emotions and needs first. It has given me the opportunity to understand what the purpose of forgiveness is. Now, after a lot of self-reflective healing work, I am grateful for everyone who challenged me on my journey to learn and practice forgiveness.

I have also come to understand that where my perspective is my truth, someone else's perspective is theirs. Even if what they do with it may be hurtful or wrong in my view. I have learned to gracefully accept that people act according to their mental and emotional state at any given time. They may have weak moments of jealousy, doubt, insecurity, or misunderstanding that I don't need to understand. I just allow things to be and assume that people tried their best, even if that didn't work too well for me. This supposition makes it easy for me to forgive.

> *"The act of forgiveness takes place in our own mind. It really has nothing to do with the other person."*
> —Louise Hay

Shouldn't you receive recognition for your brave act of forgiveness? No! It is not for others to validate. That is not the goal. This is a very private practice aimed to purify your heart. Others don't have to find out if they have been forgiven, because they may not even feel guilty in the first place. They may not think that they owe you an apology that you feel so deserving of. Isn't that mind-boggling? The story in your mind is yours and you must overcome it. If others are guilty, that is their package not yours. They may come around and they may not. Waiting for perfect closure is your emotional expectation, which will drain you.

My mom has lived an exemplary life as she embodied emotional resilience in many ways. She taught me many soul-enriching things, including letting go, forgiving, having a big heart, being the better person, and just having a beautiful kind spirit. She taught me to overlook other's mistakes and not overthink stuff. This didn't come naturally to me, so I needed some work!

You know what I did? I learned to give myself closures and that liberated me. I decided to take control of how I want to feel about a certain situation, person, or event. Allowing yourself to heal through processing your thoughts and feelings is imperative. Mindfully replaying what happened to see what lessons you can derive, is important. This might include accepting your mistakes and forgiving yourself with the intention to act better next time.

When you accept that things happened, and that you can't change that fact, the next step is to heal from it and peacefully let it go. Otherwise, your past will disturb you. You must allow some deep work within yourself to process certain things. Of course, this takes time, but way less time than holding grudges and hate towards anything or anyone.

And after you have processed and made peace with things, you come out of it much lighter and happier.

It's not an easy journey to get to a place where you forgive people. But it is such a powerful place, because it frees you!

Do I still find it hard to forgive? Any human does! It is a skill that one acquires. I go through my self-reflective mode, then process things, sit with my feelings, accept them, and reframe things in a befitting way to eventually let go. It can be hard. And it can take time. Knowing that I have learned to heal through forgiveness is comforting. I will keep challenging my practice of forgiveness and will never hold a grudge too long. The goal for me now is to reduce my processing time.

And this is exactly the step-by-step process I take my clients through. I help them reveal what's hidden within them that keeps them rooted in disempowering beliefs. I find that the more a person is willing to grow through whatever they go through, the easier they come to making peace with it through adopting forgiveness. Or else they may feel stuck in a pattern that doesn't serve them and deprives them of having control over their emotions.

Levelling Up

In essence, forgiveness requires building the courage to take the responsibility and power of a given unpleasant situation in life, reflecting and responding deliberately by choosing to free yourself of the pain. Once you get that, it will take you to another level of becoming your higher self, free of holding grudges or waiting for apologies. A self that is not in need to give explanations or expecting them. A levelled-up version of you, who is open to experiencing human emotions and allows them to pass through gracefully. You grow into someone who accepts their mistakes easily as they forgive others more. You achieve a sense of ascension with a peaceful state of mind.

Forgiving others is essential for spiritual rising. It is crucial to cleanse our hearts from any ill feelings towards others in our quest to grow spiritually. With a solid practice to forgive, your soul becomes pure and content. I've spoken to many religiously practicing people who struggle with forgiving others due to the lack of a much-needed spiritual component, which requires an internal effort to let go of the egoistic demands and adopting objectivity. There will always be triggers and situations that require you to revisit your intentions. Honour your needs and give new meanings to your personal experiences. Understand that any kind of inner work is a process and, therefore, can't be rushed.

How to Forgive

Let's embrace the fact that unless we have unfavourable things happen to us, we can't exercise the practice of forgiving. Accept all the negative situations as your chances to forgive and decide how you choose to evolve from those opportunities. With that mindset, here are some things to work on when learning how to forgive:

- Process any hurt or anger and allow yourself to understand where you come from. Validate your feelings and decide not to dwell on them too long.
- Know exactly *why* you want to forgive. Your intention to heal yourself and grow through your experiences is only for you. Forgiveness is a gift you give to yourself, and it doesn't have to be expressed to the one who hurt you or acknowledged by them.
- When you decide to heal from your hurt, you must overcome self-pity and victimization. It's important to avoid blame and your desire to understand the other person. Instead, focus on validating and understanding yourself.
- Take the responsibility for your part. In doing so, you will be able to rectify if needed and learn from your experience.
- Make excuses for others. With all compassion you can bring forth, as you forgive someone for their mistreatment towards you, know that they only showed up as best as they knew in that moment and reframe things in your favour.
- Train yourself to quickly resolve things within you. In the end, it's all a mind's game. Seek all the support you need to get there.
- Forgive as you wish to be forgiven. Pray for God's help always.

"Be merciful to others and you will receive mercy. Forgive others and Allah will forgive you."

—Prophet Muhammad (peace be on him)

Reflect

1. Think of a major situation/person you must forgive now.
2. Why do you need to forgive this?
3. How will being able to forgive impact your life positively?
1. What's keeping you stuck? Take some time to process that.
2. What action steps will you take to forgive?

Out of clutter, find simplicity. From discord, find harmony. In the middle of difficulty lies opportunity.

—Albert Einstein

Heal Your Pain

Pain is real. It is inevitable. We all have tasted it. Most of us despise our difficult times of pain, hurt, loss, rejection, loneliness, and hardship of any kind. Everyone experiences pain in different variations. But do we focus on healing our pain? Far too many people neglect the necessary healing process that helps them move on in life. If you don't heal, you remain stuck, promoting possible health problems—mental, emotional, and physical. I want to shed light on healing and give new meaning to pain. As I personally learned to heal by choosing positivity and growth in my journey, I began to accept and sweeten my relationship with pain.

Pain is something that limits you. It could be physical, emotional, or mental. If its physical, it prevents your body from optimal functioning. If it is emotional, it blocks your ability to own your true self and show up lovingly without restraints of hate, anger, resentments, jealousy, shame, etc. And mental pain, if left unattended, can hold you back massively as it may constrict and dilute your perspective and your sense of reality.

I believe healing is practiced as a lifestyle! At any given point, you required healing in some way. Every day you can practice things that have elements of healing yourself bit by bit. As you heal, you break-through your limitations and reveal what's possible for you.

Let's get a few things clear about pain. Firstly, you are not alone! Know that whatever you are going through, has been felt and shared by many others out there. So, to question, Why me? is only going to incapacitate you and victimize you. You are also not alone in having to deal with your pain. So, take control of healing your pain. It is not a weakness or shameful, as people may think, to ask for help or access resources and services that might be necessary.

Secondly, know that healing is a process. Start by accepting your pain and validating that it is difficult. It requires you to become self-aware and process how you feel. Self-compassion is a must here. Allow yourself the time to unpack, heal, and release your pain. With physical or mental pain, most people tend to *live with it* in frustration, anger, or self-pity. And with emotional pain, people jump to *moving on* without processing their pain altogether. Don't rush the healing process.

Third thing to remember is that where there is pain, there is also beauty, love, comfort, blessings, spirituality, wisdom, and so much more to be grateful for. So, staying positive is the most important tool for healing your pain.

And lastly, know that this pain will strengthen you in ways you never imagined. So much so, you will thank your painful experience after you have processed it and reframed it as you give it new meaning in your life. Your pain is here for a reason, and you must understand it as you heal.

Emotional Pain

I have experienced my share of emotional injuries such as heartbreak, disappointment, loss, loneliness, grief, and hurt, like many of you. Over time, I learned to be the alchemist and transformed my pain into purpose and my wounds into wisdom as I continue to heal. Had I not gone through my emotional setbacks, I wouldn't have learned how to forgive others, or set boundaries in my relationships, or show empathy and compassion towards myself and others, or build the passion to support others through coaching. There is no way I could gain the clarity and perspective I apply in my life today had I not endured some pain, so I'm thankful for it!

> *Pain is the fuel that lights the flame of our enlightenment.*
> —Eckhart Tolle

Understanding Emotional Pain

Whether we encounter abandonment, rejection, betrayal, loss, or any difficult life experience, such as divorce or a major accident, we need healing. Before we begin to intentionally heal emotional pain, we must understand it and frame it in a positive manner. Notice your emotional triggers, reactions, and related behaviours. Any anger, hate, fears, lack of confidence, self-doubt, shame, guilt, jealousy, unhealthy habits, insecurity, or any unsettling feelings are normally associated with some kind of emotional pain.

Hearing my clients' stories, I realize that most emotional pain can be tracked back to their younger selves. And when triggered, the unhealed wounds resurface in unexpected ways. We experience our most impactful events in childhood, when we are vulnerable and unable to make our own decisions. We seem to have no choice but to surrender, whether we understand the reasoning behind things or not. And if we are mishandled due to any circumstance, we hold on to trauma well into adulthood.

Now, as an adult, the shift needs to happen as we are responsible for healing ourselves. Such is the beauty of life! We were designed to take responsibility at some point. The longer we allow our trauma-induced negative patterns to become our norms, the more we are enslaved to the victimized programing. Our fears as a child, what we believed to be true about ourselves, who we were compared to, what was expected of us, whether we felt loved, if we were emotionally abused or abandoned, name-called or treated harshly, by anyone at all, needs to be processed as it impacts us through adulthood in ways we may be unaware of.

The way I see it now is that we were not meant to live pain-free, easy, perfect lives. We have some pain destined for us for us to grow. This is part of God's divine plan. It helps us go deeper within and heightens our awareness. Therefore, it is something that should be expected and embraced as we learn how to deal with it positively. With this mindset, we can accept any situation and allow it to transform us for the better.

Every experience in your life comes your way for a reason. Seek to learn from every painful experience and every painful interaction life sends your way. Let your pain make you better, not bitter! Use your pain as a catalyst for your transformation as opposed to becoming a victim. Accept it, process it, give it a meaning that serves you, and draw closer to God through it. Make your mess into your message! When you choose to heal, pain grows you. It makes you wiser. In that case, it can be a gift.

Processing Emotions

I have recently experienced my most painful emotional setback, and I'm adding this to a previously written chapter as if I'm journaling in my diary. I write this on day nine after my daughter got diagnosed with a life-long autoimmune condition (type 1 diabetes) which effects our whole family's daily life significantly.

As we are still wrapping our heads around what we've suddenly been struck with and what we need to do to keep her safe, with all the courage we can muster, we are still in shock, we are mourning, and we are sad. I still need to learn many things about her condition, so there are many unknowns. I feel lost and lonely, as my family and friends have no idea what we are going through. And the overwhelming sadness overtakes me when I try to imagine a lifelong struggle.

A part of me that overthinks, wants to control, and looks for answers is battling with some guilt as I keep blaming myself for not being able to prevent this from happening. I used to think that good health is about good habits and one can reverse any adverse health condition. Based on that presumption, I did everything right. Well, now I know there is this one condition that doesn't quite work that way! This has hit me hard as my girl developed the condition out of the blue. Without understanding a reason, my only option is to turn towards my spirituality for radical acceptance.

My research shows that most parents take many years to accept this diagnosis. In my case, by the will of God, I have been working on accepting it with grace and humility. If this came to me a few years back, I would have been in a very tough spot. I'm grateful for the timing at which God chose this for me. As many say, wisdom comes after age forty. This is my big forty gift, packaged in many layers for me to slowly unpack and evolve further. I'm able to process this in a healthy manner. I cry, I surrender, I embrace the journey.

It is difficult and extremely painful but I'm deeply grateful for the messages I'm receiving from above and gaining new realizations of the blessings I took for granted. Seeing your child go through a sudden, life-changing chronic condition is very difficult and the most trying thing for a parent to bear. I'm new to this and I still have an emotional healing journey ahead of me. In fact, I am releasing some feelings as I write this right now.

I'm emotionally raw but I'm also ready to do my inner work here. I want to consciously allow this to transform me for the better. There is a bigger purpose for us through this bitter reality. But first comes pain! And I'm mindful of how new this is to me. I know this needs more time and I need to be gentle with myself. I am allowing all the feelings to flow, the tough ones and the ones that bring more humility to my soul. I feel humbled to realize that I have very little control over some unknowns in my life which require my submission. What empowers me, is how I respond.

I feel immense gratitude at this trying time as it is growing my connection with my family as well as my Lord. I pray more, I show more compassion and I give more. All the things that one needs to purify one's soul have become easier for me through this painful time. Every time I see the worry on my little girl's face, I must courageously reassure her that she's safe and loved. I'm grateful to have her by my side and for the treatment that's available to manage her condition. I am suddenly her nurse, doctor, psychologist, and dietician, alongside everything I was to her prior to her diagnosis.

I have reached out for support and connected with the right resources to empower myself. I'm reframing everything to work in my favour. I will be crying in my loneliness and sharing my helplessness with Allah, which will help release difficult emotions and strengthen my soul. So, if reading this helps you reflect on anything difficult in life, I'm grateful for my vulnerability in sharing how I'm processing my emotions in my most trying time. This is as raw and honest I can be in this moment. (October, 2020)

How to Heal

First thing to understand is that, even if emotional pain comes from someone else or from something you can't control, remember, healing has to still come from you. Think about it: a person who inflicted pain upon you will never admit it to you or understand how exactly hurtful it was on the receiving end. And to expect to only heal once someone acknowledges your pain and apologizes is irrational, as it puts a lot of control for your healing in someone else's hands. Your healing is your job! This idea can be tremendously empowering for you.

Anything can become favourable to you with the correct intentions. Set the intention to heal from your emotional pain and work on the following:

- Acknowledge and validate your pain. Don't ignore it or pretend it doesn't matter. Be vulnerable to yourself so you can deal with your hurt.

- Don't depend on others to make you feel better. Choose to forgive and think about what lessons can be learned.

- Avoid replaying past events in your mind. This practice can only make you feel helpless and increases stress. The past can never be changed but can be processed with an optimistic perspective.

- Journal about your feelings to get clarity. You will be surprised at the beneficial effects of simply getting things out of your system to reflect on later—or not!

- Seek help. Whether it is a genuine friend's support, therapy, counselling, or anything that can help you heal, give yourself permission to seek it when going through any kind of pain or difficulty. Reach out to a professional to help renew your emotional health. Work with a life coach to get clarity with your mindset or gain a valuable perspective.

- Never give up on yourself. Be your biggest advocate.

Physical Pain

How you feel in your body massively determines the quality of your life! Physical pain can be debilitating, and it can really bring you down. I can share what I learned from my personal journey as I continuously strive to accept and heal my pain. There is quite a bit of physical pain that I have history with. Many people who know me don't know this about me because like most unseen conditions, chronic pain is something I suffered from silently and felt shame in sharing with others. I share my story, not to gain pity or to complain, rather, to make myself relatable to many who feel stuck in their pain stories and empower them.

I feel very strongly about this topic, as I was the one in my family who went through the most broken bones, accidents, surgeries, and some related limitations, inflammatory issues, and muscular/nerve pain. Also, as a sensitive feeler, some emotional hurt showed up in my body in the form of pain.

Now, of course, pain can be much worse, however, when we speak of validating pain, we don't compare. Anytime someone says to you, "Well, look at so-and-so and this could be worse," know that they are not going to hold space for you to share your story, so be cautious. No wonder so many people are hesitant to speak up about their pain and are shy to seek help. They are compared and ridiculed for sharing their comparatively "lesser" problems. This is why I feel such discomfort writing about my physical pain even now and I have revisited the vulnerable areas in this book to make sure my purpose of sharing is clear and delivers a helpful message.

Let's avoid belittling and dismissing pain! When we want to solve problems, we begin by acknowledging the problem, big or small. There is no pain competition. We all want to heal our pain and live our lives gracefully. We should all strive to function in the most optimal physical state possible. Pain should be something we actively attempt to manage. It can adversely impact our moods, functionality, mental health, lifestyle, and relationships.

Yes, we can always feel grateful for not having it worse. But that is not going to heal us. Healing requires validation and nurturing of our feelings, followed with action. Also, be conscious not to only *complain* about your pain, rather seek to *heal*. So, a great tip for anyone wanting to support another person through anything difficult is to hold space for them non-judgmentally and listen. It is good to validate that what someone may be going through is difficult for them. Just listening can be a big help for someone wanting to be seen and heard.

Story Time

Let me share a bit of my pain story! When I was twenty, I got into a major car accident. I was hit at high speed and thrown off to the opposite window, shattering it as well as my humerus (upper arm bone) into many pieces. I had a major surgery on my right arm and was hospitalized for two weeks, followed by a long healing process with much discomfort, pain, and limitation. As a result, my whole left side of the body was impacted. I still ended up keeping the two plates in my arm, which cause me chronic pain. Things could have been much worse, so I share this with immense gratitude in my heart.

I am right-handed, so for over six months, I wasn't able to write, drive, or do simple tasks that required more dominant-hand effort. I became ambidextrous during this phase, which was a good thing. I had no clue about how much physiotherapy was required and completely ignored the proper protocol needed to gain back my strength in the arm. It was advised to remove the plates in my arm in a couple years, but I dint prioritise that. I didn't bother to notice any other pain related to the whiplash from being hit at high speed. I was just eager to go back to university and finish my semester.

I was young, so I healed quick enough (or so I thought,) resumed life, and put the whole event behind my back without giving it much thought or processing any related trauma. As years went by, the aches and pains began to creep up on me, along with emotional triggers. I had constant back pain, hip misalignment issues, sciatica, intense neck and shoulder pain, and occasional inflammation and pain in my arm whenever it was overworked. I had four pregnancies with chronic pain issues as I suffered in silence, feeling lonely and helpless. I was told by my doctor that it must be the accident that caused all the pain and all I could do was manage it with painkillers. I felt like a victim. Until I had the accident to blame, I had a bad relationship with my pain.

For my family and friends, that major car accident was a mere memory of calling or visiting me at the hospital. After I was discharged and visibly recovered, it was just me, left all alone, in my body, to cope with what followed. For the longest time after my accident, I dealt with my own pain story. A story that made me feel ashamed, unheard, and vulnerable.

The closest people to me never knew I was suffering with chronic pain. I felt ashamed of bringing it up as I feared invalidation or insensitive reactions from others. I thought I was too young to have pain in my body. For years, I had a history of pain haunting me in various ways. Sometimes, I fell into self-pity, other times I went into my own shell. The worst was becoming accustomed to pain and accepting it as my normal. I developed a higher threshold for pain, but it made me frustrated and moody. I was clueless about how to manage this pain. I blamed the accident and felt helpless. By telling myself that story on repeat, I lost a lot of my power to change my situation. I needed a big *inner shift*.

I had to learn to forgive and let go of what happened to me and fully accept it. Islamically speaking, any pain one suffers from, is rewarded in the hereafter if endured with patience. This concept can provide inner strength and comfort; however, it doesn't solve the problem or improve one's standard of living.

Chronic pain can be draining and impacts one's mental and emotional health. I needed to empower myself by learning about alternative ways to manage my pain. I began to tune in to my emotions more as I discovered how physical pain is connected to emotional pain. Blaming and avoiding was not an option once I decided to embrace my body as it was and began to positively manage my pain. I needed to reprogram my relationship with pain.

Once my kids were out of diapers, I began to work towards healing and managing my pain actively. Along with a lot of inner emotional healing work, I invested in regular shockwave treatments, practicing yoga, physiotherapy/chiropractic care, massage, meditation, breathwork, and healthy nutrition. I prioritized my physical health consciously. I may not fully reverse what's injured, but I can strengthen and take good care of my physical being with compassion and awareness.

What I find is that most people don't actively work on the root causes of their pain. They don't wish to change their lifestyles or habits such as diet or exercise. People want to continue to live the way they do and complain about pain or limitations as they rely on pain killers. I decided to not become dependent on narcotics for my pain and instead add more super foods to my diet with anti-inflammatory properties and health benefits. Three things I can say: Food is medicine. Movement is compulsory. Nature heals. So, get your sunshine, eat healing foods, and exercise regularly, if you want to deal with your pain actively.

The major accident is just one of a few of my physical pain stories. From debilitating chronic wrist pain from a ganglion cyst (needing surgery) to years of excruciating abdominal pain due to a bad case of adenomyosis (also needing a hysterectomy), I've dealt with my fair share of pain in my body. A few years back, I had a bad fall on my hip, which requires strength training and is yet another ongoing healing journey for me. I cannot compromise my body by indulging in practices that adversely affect my pain. I have adopted to doing everything in my power to help my physical pain so I can enjoy the standard of life I desire. As a result, I am grateful for the results and the renewed sense of appreciation for my body, by the Grace of God.

Healing Mindset

When you are suffering from any kind of physical pain, it can raise expectations from others. You expect others to somehow understand you or cater towards you. This mindset can be very limiting and disappointing. You will never be able to get anyone to understand how you feel. After all, this is your experience, not theirs. When you choose self-pity or codependency, the expectation is that someone else needs to validate, sympathize, or help *fix* things for you. Such a victimized perspective only hurts you and deprives you of recovering. What you need is a *healing mindset*. One that empowers you and allows you to take charge of your well-being.

One needs to also understand that humans feel and process pain in a very personal way. Some people feel pain much more and others feel it much less than you. Everyone processes it differently as well. Some of us like to go deeper with our pain and might experience it on many levels while others jump to problem-solving way quicker and avoid dealing with any deep stuff altogether. People will not understand your pain and you may not understand theirs. Stop expecting your family or friends to understand or validate you or help you in managing your pain. If their comments or invalidation trigger you in any way, do yourself a favour and avoid bringing it up to them altogether. If they provide safe spaces for you to share and talk, great, otherwise, keep expectations low.

Reach out to professionals or support groups or like-minded people who have either experienced or have expertise regarding what you're going through. Opening up to the right people for a much-needed heart-to-heart can help you heal. Know who to share and be vulnerable with.

Develop a healing mindset regarding your pain. Regardless of what kind of pain it is, your mindset about it matters the most. Are you feeling like it's unfair? Or do you think that you don't have enough information to feel empowered to supported? Bringing strength from within to cope with your condition is key. Do research to attain the knowledge you might need to empower yourself. Having pain and choosing to suffer are two separate things. And rejecting or not accepting your pain altogether is an act lead by your ego. Your ego is what questions your pain and asks, Why me?

I adopted a strategy that I also teach my clients called *reframing*. It is my favourite neuro-linguistic programing (NLP) technique. Basically, any situation in life can be reframed to work in our favour. Thinking, How is what's happening good for me? Learning how to train our minds to habitually begin to think positively about things that happens to us can be a remarkable thinking habit. Growth occurs after well-processed pain.

We all know how a caterpillar transforms into a butterfly through a painful process. It must sit inside a chrysalis and hang off a twig alone for days to do the painful inner work. After spinning itself a silky cocoon, within its protective casing, the caterpillar must go through a self-destructive process only to regrow new parts in solitude and radically transform its body. Finally breaking through its barrier and emerging as a gorgeous creature, completely different from the caterpillar. This evolution occurs under immense pressure and symbolizes the potential of pain. The butterfly takes flight and shares its beauty after having gone through enormous self-transformation.

A healing mindset embraces setbacks, sorrows, losses, sickness, or pain with courage. Everyone has pain in life. However, people who have a healing mindset look for ways to evolve through pain. It has profound meaning for them. Sometimes, it serves as a gentle reminder. Other times, it brings a transformative, life-changing kind of lesson that shifts things on a much larger scale. It can be truly powerful when you decide to turn your pain into purpose.

> *The ego says, "I shouldn't have to suffer," and that thought makes you suffer so much more. It is a distortion of the truth, which is always paradoxical. The truth is that you need to say yes to suffering before you can transcend it.*
> —Eckhart Tolle

You Are Not Your Pain

Many people develop an association with their pain. Your struggle might be a catalyst for a big change in your life, but it certainly does not define you. Your understanding of your pain must be greater than your attachment to it. Pain can be very debilitating as it promotes sadness and can make you feel lonely or depressed at times. You must experience it without letting it overpower you.

Separate *who you are* from your pain. Observe the course of negative thoughts that might run through your mind. See yourself as the one who's witnessing all the emotional pain or physical discomfort. But don't allow it to overtake your life or define who you are. When you're attached to your pain, your desire to change the past becomes greater than your desire to heal. As it's nature, pain already comes with the possibility to heal.

> *For indeed, with hardship comes ease.*
> —Qur'an 94:5

Self-empowerment is the answer! Along with a nurturing support system and healing plan that you create for yourself, a good amount of will power is much needed. Most physical conditions can be either reversed or managed. When you decide to heal yourself and take necessary action, you will stop complaining and self-victimizing. You will search for solutions for your condition and shift your mind towards healing. And perhaps as you heal yourself, you might be inspired to support others and create an impact much bigger than yourself. Pain is the gift that can create impact which reaches far and beyond oneself.

Healing Physical Pain

With a positive *healing mindset*, here are some tips for physical healing:

- Create your healing plan which includes attention to diet, sleep, and managing stress levels—three areas where inflammation develops (according to my naturopath). A lack of attention to any of these can slow down the healing process.
- Exercise regularly. Moving is very beneficial for sending the signals to the cells in your body to start the healing process.
- Learn everything in your power to help yourself heal. Try new modalities or remedies to help your pain.
- Ask for help and talk about how you feel. Reach out to therapists, coaches, and counsellors, and build a support system.
- Cut down on physically draining tasks that should not be on your priority list. Mindfully choose where you engage and preserve your energy.
- Take the time to be alone with yourself to rest and recover. Solitude is great for reflective work, to connect with God, and enhance spirituality.

Reflect

1. Think about an unhealed wound from the past, an emotional, mental, or physical struggle, or any painful condition you currently live with right now. Reflect on how it limits you.

2. After reading this chapter, what are some of the ways you will take responsibility for healing your pain?

3. Make three clear intentions and write them down.

It's not what you look at that matters. It's what you see.

—Henry David Thoreau

Get Over Judgements

Our judgements about life, ourselves, situations, or others impact our outcomes immensely. How we perceive everything and what kind of mindset we develop needs to be observed with curiosity and perhaps even questioned and shifted.

Many situations in our lives can be good or bad, simply depending on how we judge them. Most times, we make our judgements based on our previous limited exposure and resulting biased opinions. How we view things matters immensely as we explore options and opportunities in our lives. Any person can appear good or bad. We may judge them based on what we hear or assume. An act can be good or bad, but wait, before I go on, why don't we cross out the idea of labelling everything as "good" or "bad"? How about learning to allow some space for curiosity and exploring the what ifs? That is where your mind produces magic! That is where you create space for possibility and potential.

Our judgements drive how we feel about ourselves or others. How good am I? How capable am I? Am I enough? Our true essence revolves around our judgements of ourselves. Let's begin to wonder about whether these judgements are even true. Where did they come from? And what they mean for us. How can we overcome our negative judgements about ourselves? I'm provoking your mind to think in unique ways to ask some simple question about yourself and how you think and feel, as these simple questions may be the answers to why some things may be difficult for you. You'll find that you are your biggest limitation that stands in your way.

We judge ourselves and others in harsh ways all the time. Mostly, such judgements lead to misunderstandings and negativity. I would love to be able to claim that I am such a wonderful, open-minded, warm person, that I don't judge anyone, but that's just not the truth. I am also hard on myself, and I have high expectations, which tempts me to judge others as well. However, with conscious inner shifting, such instances have considerably lessened.

I'm not referring to constructive criticism or healthy advice. It is negative assessments that we allow ourselves to establish on a regular basis, even if we don't express them. Just having judgemental thoughts can do its damage to our way of thinking. Judgements about how other people live, how they behave, whether they are happy, how they may see us, what success means to them, what choices they make, or our limited ideas on status consciousness and ignorant comparisons, etc. If you want an upgraded version of yourself, you must work on getting over such judgements.

Becoming mindful of our negative judgements towards others and understanding the origins of our perspectives can allow us to become more open-minded and trustworthy as we don't project our presumptions onto others. This way, we create safe spaces to connect and become curious about ourselves, others, and life's possibilities.

Why do we Judge?

Well, there could be many psychological reasons for why we judge, but the truth is that it has everything to do with our own selves. At times, we might feel insecure in some way and thinking of others as "less than" ourselves makes us feel better in comparison. Sometimes, we judge when someone is different or not relatable to us. We simply don't understand them, so we judge. There could be jealousy at play at times. You don't see things happening for yourself, so you judge those who have something you don't. You may diminish other's efforts, invalidate their pain, dismiss their achievements, or label them and harden your heart in the process. Not a peaceful place to be!

Our company plays a huge part in what we do. We could pick up the bad habit of jumping to conclusions about others if that is what we are mostly exposed to. If we are surrounded by people who constantly pass judgements on others, we will adopt similar behaviour. People gossip because they judge others. They develop an understanding of others which they talk about negatively in their absence, a behaviour that can really pollute the soul.

It's all in your perspective. At times, we are labelled as being too sensitive while we judge others to be too harsh. If you notice, our expectations are also at play. Occasionally, we are guilty of hurting others' feelings and yet we jump to label them to be sensitive. Other times, we expect others to simply understand us and not take our hurtful words seriously, because of course, we are joking! Remember, hurtful or sarcastic remarks are never funny. A lot of our assumptions and judgements tend to be inaccurate and may create misunderstandings and further problems in our relationship as well as turmoil within ourselves.

Many of our judgmental encounters come through comparing ourselves to others. We all have experienced growth in life at various things. Whenever we progress in life in any way, we are hit with a sense of superiority regarding it. Sometimes, even in your spiritual growth, where you feel like you have understood something on a deeper level more than others. It could be your knowledge or a life experience that grants you more confidence in certain areas which puts you in a position to look down upon others who may not have what you have. This is when our egoistic tendencies project our superiorities upon others.

Knowing too much can be difficult. So, the more you know, the more you are tempted to judge others. Take your growth spurts as opportunities to work on your attitude and be humble. Understand that you have a heavier responsibly when you know more. And this is enough reason for you to provide a non-judgmental space for others behind you, with humility.

Similarly, many may feel far too behind in their knowledge or experience, which then causes them to make inaccurate assumptions, judgements, or expectations. In such instances, you may feel insecure or overwhelmed, but be inspired to learn from those who have acquired what you seek. Don't judge what you see in them, become curious about their journey instead. And allow yourself to tap into your own potential.

Our unawareness of our impulsive judgements can do a lot of damage to our personal development.

There could be different motivations behind our judging tendencies, and it is important to bring awareness to them so we can work on avoiding this pattern. There is something that needs to be uncovered for you on a deeper level. Whatever you put out to the world, you attract yourself. It is the *law of attraction*. Instead of choosing to understand, you choose judgement. That negative energy goes around and comes back to haunt you in various ways.

It's about You!

I have my moments where I am prompted to make judgements, but I have developed conscious awareness of it. The more I work on myself, the more I become aware of myself and less judging of others. The times I detach myself from the ego and attach to my soul, I feel no need to make judgements of others or even myself.

The thing is, anything we want to correct within ourselves requires self-work. Taking responsibility of our thoughts is vital. When our brain is programed to produce *automatic negative thoughts,* also known as our ANTs, most things in life become negative. We can overcome this pattern by genuinely challenging our mind and training it to think positively. Soon enough, that becomes our automatic response.

This applies to you underestimating yourself or dismissing a situation or person altogether, which can become very limiting for you to aim higher for yourself. It can also limit your understanding of the world around you. Try to wonder what prompts you to jump to negative conclusions and nudge yourself to think of the opposite being equally probable. Your automatic responses should not be believed as they may not even be true.

In a spiritual context, any negative exchange with others is rusty for the soul and requires purification in order to live soulfully. When we accept ourselves and begin to love who we are, the need to judge others diminishes. How we show up in life through projecting what we think or feel about others has a lot to do with who we happen to be in that moment. You judge others based on your own egoistic inclinations, insecurities, jealousies, comparisons, or attachments to your stubborn ideas. It really is all about you!

The more comfortable you become with yourself, the more neutrally you'll see others. After all, that is how you want others to see you. You want them to give you grace and allow room for mistakes. As you adopt flexibility towards yourself, you will begin to project the same onto others.

Observe with Curiosity

Anytime we are neutral, without any presumptions or notions about anyone or anything in life, we show up with more curiosity. We can then ask intelligent questions and allow ourselves to explore concepts, emotions, and possibilities. Just noticing and understanding our judgemental stories that our mind rapidly comes up with, will make us more emotionally intelligent and open minded.

> *The ability to observe without evaluating is the highest form of intelligence.*
> —Jiddu Krishnamurti

Observe, listen, pause, and make humble inquiries to understand and find unconventional solutions to anything. It always feels good when you purposely avoid judging and remain open.

This practice can improve our connections and people skills. You'll find that when you're at a happy place, you experience more self-control and that is where there's lesser room for judgement. On the flip side, when we judge others, we are left with the related ill-feelings. We end up taking on the burden of that judgement.

To become your better version, you need to avoid looking at someone else in a negative light. You're not in their situation, you don't have their life, and you don't understand them nearly enough to pass a judgement in any way. Also, understand that your judgement of them doesn't affect them in the least bit, because it may not be true. What you perceive to be true is a creation of your mind and you must take full responsibility for generating your negative thoughts.

Allow yourself to get curious about your thoughts and overcome any negative judgements by using a cognitive behavioural therapy (CBT) technique I learned from my therapist. It's called the *C-cubed rule.* Whenever you are judgemental towards others or yourself, try to *catch, check, and change* the thought. Basically, you *catch* yourself noticing your thoughts and behaviours that project judgement. Then *check* to see where they come from internally, or at least question to see if they are true based on any solid reasoning or evidence. And finally *change* them to neutral or even positive non-judging thoughts.

This is not to say that we become gullible and let serious things slide. Sometimes, we need to see red flags in certain situations and make the correct judgements. Other times, we need to honour our intuitive hesitations and instant gut feelings, which may come about naturally and are not based on our judging habits. There are limitations for everyone to draw boundaries when it comes to giving benefit of the doubt. Never allow your kindness to be misused against you, yet also resist judging too quickly. The middle path is optimal in almost any situation.

People function based on how they feel. Even the person who appears to be insensitive or harsh has a deeper unhealed reality. Just be curious and open-minded. So, if we were to truly show up as our *higher selves*, we could really overlook certain things and stay grounded in our own reality. It protects us from getting too offended by a lot of things. Because everyone shows up as good as they are capable of, based on who they are deep inside at any given moment.

How to Stop Judging

Start by understanding that the act of negative judgment is harmful, whether it is towards oneself, a situation, or others. Bring awareness towards where your thoughts originate from. Here are some things to consider working on:

- Observe your thoughts. Monitor your negative judgments and work on pushing them towards positive. If it is hard at first, begin by being neutral about things. An easy way is to assume that you don't know enough about any situation and remain open to possibility.

- Look for good in yourself, others, and different situations. Focus on positivity and remain unbiased and curious.
- Focus on yourself. Get busy with monitoring your own intentions, thoughts, feelings, goals, and conduct.
- Do some *shadow work*. We all have our dark sides. As you explore yours, you'll stop making assumptions about others and/or projecting negatively onto them.

Non-Judgemental Support

As a person from the community of service in the emotional space, I know this firsthand that when I am hard on myself, I end up judging and criticizing myself strictly. This can be difficult when we hold space for others and encourage vulnerability yet forget to practice what we preach ourselves. It is a hard thing to offer when we are so fixated on showing up strongly for others and neglecting ourselves in the process. I encourage you to bring awareness towards showing up for others with your cup full.

Supporting others non-judgementally can be a mandatory skill to learn in life. Anyone going through a tough time needs support without the worries of being judged. We as humanity struggle with holding such spaces for others to share freely and courageously. More and more people today feel lonely and distant from one another due to the fear of judgement. We need to allow people to feel guarded and safe to share their stories with us as we build deeper connections.

Through my journey of coaching, I've learned to become aware of my intentions and motivations for helping others. Any chapter in anyone's life is a remarkable story of pain, opportunity, and growth. And when you see life in those terms, there is no room for judgement. We are only doing the best we are capable of at any given time. And what we need is non-judgemental support. Some of us grow faster than others and we should respectfully allow everyone their own pace. An open mind can really become your strongest gift.

Give others as well as yourself some slack. We are meant to fall short at times. We need to have setbacks for growth to occur. Learn to admire whatever you encounter and give beautiful positive meanings to everything from your generous and creative lens.

Reflect

1. Notice your thoughts for a week and catch yourself when you have judging thoughts about others, or even yourself. Write them down.

2. Think about why you judge someone negatively. Where did it come from within you? (i.e., insecurity, expectation, competition? etc.)

3. How will you reframe your judging thought into a neutral one or possibly a positive one? Practice and notice your progress.

Comparison is the thief of joy.

—Theodore Roosevelt

Stop Comparison

Your life is unique to you. It is unmatched with anyone else's in the entire world. Your situation, talents, goals, and path are entirely unique to you and your purpose in this world among many other things. There is only one of you! How amazing is that? And yet, how many of us are busy comparing our lives to others or are in competition with others? It is a toxic habit most people are enslaved to, which makes them unhappy, stuck, and feeling like they are not *good enough*.

With the amount of our exposure to social media, it's easier than ever to constantly find someone better to compare ourselves with, which only serves to make us feel bad about ourselves. Once we go down that road, we never find an end. The tendency to compare ourselves to others is a human emotion and also a choice. Many of us have adopted this habit, which steals joy from our lives. We must challenge ourselves to break the cycle of hurting ourselves through comparison with others, we will become much more peaceful and happier.

Scarcity Mindset

The worse thing about comparing with others is that your focus is on the wrong person! You can only be in charge of one life—yours. But when we constantly compare ourselves to others, we waste our time and energy focusing on other people's lives rather than our own. We develop a *scarcity mindset*, living with *what is not* rather than appreciating and working on *what is.* Seeing the glass half empty rather than the glass half full.

Comparisons often result in resentments, towards others and ourselves. We don't grow green grass by focusing on our neighbour's garden, we do it by nurturing our own. So, instead of wasting time comparing your path to someone else's, spend it on investing, creating, and caring for your own.

In my conversations with people, the feeling of *not being enough* often shows up due to comparisons with others. One is fresh in my mind where a client of mine, in her mid-forties, decided to give up because she wasn't where other women of the same age in her life were. She perceived herself as a failure due to persistent thoughts about where she *should* have been in her personal or career life according to her perceived *timeline*. She completely overlooked and invalidated her own struggles that she had overcome. Her own life was of inspirational value to many, but she chose to focus on remaining frustrated and feeling incompetent due to comparisons with others her age.

Over a session with me, she experienced her biggest *inner shift* when I called her out on this bizarre idea of comparing herself to others. During our session together, I could tell that she had expected me to help her match up to those she compared herself to. Or maybe she wanted me to validate her feelings of being *behind* in comparison with others. But with all good intentions, I had a different perspective for her to reflect on altogether. I asked her basic questions about her strengths and her "whys" and her values in life. And it was surprising for her to discover that she had no idea what drove her in life, why she felt the way she did, and how she was going to change. She was clueless about her direction in life, as she was busy noticing others.

This was our breakthrough moment! We needed to empower her through personal discovery while mindfully shifting her focus on her own life, where it needs to be for any progress to occur. After realizing that her actual version of reality is so different from the one she created through societal pressures and comparisons, she felt a heavy release and a new surge of excitement. It was priceless! We worked on de-programing her habit of comparing herself to others, who were only her competition in her mind. That distorted notion needed to be erased in order to bring attention towards her unique path.

The whole idea that if someone else got more than you then you don't have enough, is flawed. Someone else's success shouldn't affect yours too much more than a motivational boost or an inspirational guide. And there is an abundant feeling that follows when you truly learn to achieve and celebrate your own life goals on your terms. Where there is an inner abundant feeling, there can't be scarcity. You cultivate abundance from within, free of comparisons or irrelevant measuring sticks.

Shifting the Paradigm

Sometimes, our negative patterns are picked up in our early years and require some healing work. I do this work with other women because I went through a similar struggle. I grew up with comparisons to my siblings and competition with classmates. Being compared to them on how well I did in school, or how fast I finished any task. Or if I could learn something as quickly as them. What position I ranked at in my grade was of extreme importance. You notice the pattern? I was programed to defeat others, to be number one in my class . . . and if I didn't, well, then I was shamed and not *good enough.*

In all the comparison and competition, I lost myself—my true essence, my purpose, my authentic spirit, my voice, and my gifts. I had to work really hard to reclaim all that. And my journey of *shifting inwards* took a lot of letting go of who I saw myself as through other people's eyes and building my self-esteem through who I saw myself to be on a deeper level.

The problem lies within the eye of the perceiver. Ultimately, how we see things is what is most important. Getting fixated on what others accomplish or where they are in life compared to you can be a self-destructive obsession, which can make you lose perspective of your own reality in life. It is a sure-fire recipe for a drop in self-confidence and happiness.

Instead of comparing and feeling *not good enough*, if you look at your strengths, your choices, your circumstances, and the efforts you have put in based on your unique style and ability, you'll see that you have a lot to offer and a lot to be happy about. Being able to look at your own strengths and see your true value is one of the keys to success, because without this ability, you won't believe in yourself and be demotivated.

When we are happy with ourselves, we set achievable goals. And when we are beating ourselves down, we feel incompetent and are unable to set those goals. We need to overcome external irrelevant distractions and honour our individual selves.

> *Today you are you, that is truer than true. There is no one alive who is you-er than you.*
> —Dr. Seuss

Why Stop Comparing?

Firstly, because it is usually an unfair comparison to start with. We typically compare mindlessly to the worst we know of ourselves to the best we presume about others. There will always be those who are better, and those who are worse than you. Where you are on the ladder of accomplishments or strengths in life has got nothing to do with someone else's. A comparison drawn just for the sake of matching up to others without reason, can instill feelings of frustration and can distort your reality as well as the reality of others. Such a comparison is pointless.

Secondly, even if you feel like you do well in comparison with others, you may enjoy a momentary ego boost, but it doesn't get you very far in life. You might become arrogant as you look down upon others. Also, comparing yourself with other's faults, misfortune, or failures to make yourself feel better can also be unhealthy for you if your intention is simply to "look better." Feeling good about yourself should have nothing to do with how others are doing unless the intention is to feel grateful. Humility must be paired with our accomplishments, so we can be charismatic and inspire others.

And lastly, if you feel behind in comparison, you build resentment, which saddens you. It can also plague your heart with jealousy, which is unhealthy for the soul. Question why you feel behind? Who's keeping track of the measure for what's good enough for you in relation to that other person? Are you comparing only aspects of others that appear better than yours? In that case, there may be aspects of you that are better than them? So, what is your purpose for comparing?

Any way you look at comparisons with others, you realize that it doesn't benefit you, unless it inspires you.

Comparison as Inspiration

Inspiration comes with positivity and requires action. When you set your goals, yes, look for inspiration from others. But not to feel behind, rather, to work toward your goals.

Look at *what* you're comparing. Are you looking at the external, materialistic gains of others? How they look, dress, or what they own? Or are you looking for their character that they have built? If you're focused on the images of people's lives based on what you see on the social media or what you presume their lives look like based on your imaginations, then it will impact your self-worth and happiness adversely. Any time you feel unhappy about a comparison with others, it is not good for you.

However, if you are inspired by their positive outlook, pleasant demeanor, confidence, or kindness, allow that to be a catalyst for change in your own life. Try to replicate their journey and exemplify good characteristics of others. Whatever inspires you about others, find out how they got there and what version of achieving something you admire in others is possible for you. We are supposed to look for great examples in others to try to adopt greatness ourselves. Everything you wish to achieve has already been achieved by someone else out there. Follow their path. Get curious about the journey instead of getting too fixated on what the outcome looks like compared to your present reality.

Also, there is such a thing called *healthy competition*. In Islam, it is encouraged to "compete for more good deeds" such as trying to give more in charity etc. You could have productive competitions at home as you race to build better habits together. You may even compete while playing games etc. It may be healthy for learning skills, sharpen our minds, and keeping up the motivation.

To have our human inclination to compare with others from time to time is natural. But to become aware and use such comparisons towards our benefit is the needed *inner shift*. Focus your attention entirely on your life goals using others' examples as your motivation. This can be more authentic and exciting for you. Notice your growth and compare yourself to your old self. Doesn't it make much more sense to compare to the only person who has lived in your shoes? We want to strive to be the best possible versions of ourselves. Commit to growing a little bit each day and enjoy the little advancements you make without comparing your path to others.

How to Stop Comparing

If comparing with others makes you feel overwhelmed, here are a few tips to overcome this habit:

- Notice your own success and pursue it further. Validate your struggles and triumphs. Avoid getting distracted by someone else's path that may seem similar to yours. Believe me, it never is!

- Limit social media usage if it prompts you to compare with random people. Unfollow any accounts that trigger you. Use your time to build yourself up. Instead of over-consuming comparative content, start *creating* your own reality.

- Find inspiration without comparison. Appreciate and compliment others openheartedly. This habit can help you become genuinely inspired by another instead of feeling insecure or threatened. Get curious and humbly ask for advice from those you admire.

- Practice gratitude. Appreciate and acknowledge where you are and what you have in your life.

- Focus on your capacity and ambition instead of incompetency. Notice your potential and grow it.

- Compare with yourself instead of others. Are you a better version of yourself than last year? Are you trying to evolve into your personal best? Become obsessed with working on yourself. If you keep moving forward, you're successful.

Reflect

1. What are some ways you compare yourself to others?
2. What do you notice about others the most?
3. Who inspires you to be better and why?
4. List a few ways to shift your focus on your own goals.

Healthy striving is self-focused:"How can I improve?" Perfectionism is other-focused: "What will they think?"

—Brené Brown

Conquer Perfectionism

When I was younger, I remember living in fear of messing up. The insecurity of not getting the approval of those in authority got me striving for perfection. I felt as if making mistakes was shameful, which created intense anxiety for me at a young age. I developed the traits of perfectionism and used it as a shield to hide my fears. I didn't enjoy making high grades or being a position holder any much more than getting approval for it. It felt like a loss of effort after I got a few praiseworthy words in return, as I continued to maintain the false image and struggled aimlessly. I think I missed out on the joy of the *process* of reaching any such goal. My curious mind just couldn't understand and connect with what was to be pursued and that created a void within me.

Growing up, as much as I credit and appreciate my dad for his high standards as a parent, I learned that the only way to receive validation from him was to be a high achiever. Getting a grade less than an A made me feel like a failure. And I never quite understood the struggle, the rat race, to get to the end with flying colours. It wasn't inspiring for me to simply prove myself to be the best of the lot. Where was it going to benefit me? Why was I in such competition with others? What did I need to prove to myself and others? As a child, I needed that communicated to me for my inquisitive nature in order to develop authenticity.

Achieving good grades is healthy if you study the material and enjoy the learning experience as much as your high grades. One needs to understand their goals before aiming to achieve them. For me, it was a constant pressure, not something I understood or enjoyed. Pursuing excellence and aiming high is great, but not merely in a few school subjects. There are many other areas that one can excel in life far more authentically and purposefully than competing with classmates over Math grades. What else was important in life? I don't remember! There was a lack of balance in my little mind, with a strict focus on achieving grades that got me acceptance.

If a child is only rewarded for high achievement, over time, they learn that their value as a person depends on being perfect. Whenever I fell short, I felt like I was not good enough. My passions and intelligence were left unexplored and ignored. I couldn't tap into my unique talents as I was busy maintaining appearances and competing with others over things that weren't my strengths or interests. Wanting to hide my imperfections and showing up as well-put-together became an inauthentic way of portraying myself. I learned to be hard on myself and became my worst critic. This deadly pattern continued until college years and still shows up for me now as a "recovering perfectionist."

Understanding Perfectionism

In my freshman year of college, I took a public speaking course. I had serious anxiety getting up in front of an audience to give a speech due to my perfectionist attitude. The first assignment given to us in class was to present an informative speech. I decided to speak about perfectionism as I had just discovered my own struggle. I wanted to share about the painful reality of this acquired trait. As I researched and spoke about the topic, I remember experiencing a release and deciding to do something about it. I knew this would take some healing work and I had to dig deep and get to the bottom of things. It has ever since been a continuous battle to defeat perfectionism and become more soulfully aligned.

> *Perfectionism is a self-destructive and addictive belief system that fuels this primary thought: If I look perfect, and do everything perfectly, I can avoid or minimize the painful feelings of shame, judgment, and blame.*
>
> —Brené Brown, *The Gifts of Imperfection* (Brown, Gifts of Imperfection 2010)

Here are a few myths I discovered on my path to recovery from perfectionism. Firstly, perfectionism is not the same as *excellence*. We are unintentionally sold the concept of perfection with the distorted understanding that we are pursuing excellence, which is a lie! In reality, it is a fear-based response to insecurity that is learned at a young age. Excellence is a standard we set for ourselves to apply ourselves fully and feel accomplished upon reaching. Perfectionism, on the other hand, asks you to reach a certain standard to prove yourselves. Big difference!

Secondly, you grow up with the belief that generally likeable traits such as being a good leader, having a keen eye for detail, having high standards, working in a structured and organized manner, not making mistakes, etc. *makes* you a perfectionist. Not at all! Those could be your good personality traits based on other factors in your upbringing. However, there are completely different motivations behind one's perfectionistic inclinations.

And lastly, perfectionism is not something you are born with. It is a pattern that we acquire mostly due to our unhealthy programing in childhood. If you are neurodivergent such as ADHD, you might struggle with perfectionism.

Perfectionism is a word we throw around a lot, and it's been turned into a positive trait most of times, which confuses people. There are a few false beliefs disguised behind perfectionism, which is why most people are either in denial of it or they hide behind fake messaging of their minds.

You tell yourself, I'm a perfectionist because I'm diligent and sensible. No! You're a perfectionist because you can't stop second-guessing and doubting yourself. You've probably also developed the habit of "overthinking" because of it. You think to yourself, I'm a perfectionist because I have high standards. Not exactly! You might just have unrealistic expectations of yourself and a fear of failure. You might think, I'm a perfectionist because I like things done properly, neatly, or in an organized fashion. Wrong again! You are a control freak and that's why you are a perfectionist. Sorry! Hard pill to swallow for me too at times! But those are some *truth bombs*!

You might think, Well I'm not necessarily a typical "perfectionist" per se, but I like to get things done right! Be careful, as there is a fine line. Still, explore why you must do things at someone's standard of *good enough*. If it is a standard you set for yourself, question why. Go ahead... Do things right, in fact do them with excellence, but don't make *no mistakes* and *perfection* the only standards for yourself as they will impact you when you get stuck in unnecessary time-consuming tasks. As a result, you become an *all or none* kind of person with less flexibility. And you may delay tasks because of the burden of doing things perfectly.

See, knowing where to give extra time and attention to detail is important when you are mindfully aware of it. But your autopilot response to things should not be, I'll do it when I can do it perfectly; rather, I'll do it as good as I can *now*. Taking imperfect action is way better than waiting for the right time to do things perfectly. This *inner shift* will begin to make the big difference.

> *Perfectionism is a loop ... an obsessive, debilitating closed system that causes you to get stuck in the details and to lose sight of the whole. Perfectionism is the ego's wicked demand.*
>
> —Julia Cameron, *The Artist's Way*

As an artist myself, I understand my perfectionistic inclinations very well. I rarely felt excited to do my projects when I was leading with the fear of messing up or not doing it according to some fabricated standard. Perfectionism can be the opposite of humility, which allows us to move slowly and steadily forward, learning from our mistakes. It deprives us of enjoying the process. Bottom line is that perfectionism keeps you stuck. It can be the killer of your dreams. It's not a strength!

You develop *procrastination* as a symptom of perfectionism. Because many of us are so petrified of bloopers that we can't begin a new project until we know that we can do it perfectly. Many times, this means that we never begin it or take longer to be ready to get started. And while perfectionism absolutely gets in the way of living a courageous and wholesome life, there's good news: in due time, you can conquer it!

Recovering from Perfectionism

The key to shifting anything internally is gaining deep awareness. Bringing more and more understanding towards your tendencies and the effects they have on your life is a necessary starting point. Many traits of perfectionism evolve in our lifetime as we grow into it. Begin to get clarity around the concept and understand why perfectionism is a killer.

I read somewhere that, "clarity breeds mastery." In order to begin some real work around my perfectionism, I needed to gain clarity. I grew up thinking of perfectionism as a positive attribute until I began to gain awareness around the pain that hides behind it. When you find yourself thinking in terms of "good enough" you know you are in dangerous territory. It comes down to your intentions and what drives you to be a certain way. There is *fear*, *insecurity*, and *ego* at play.

When overcome by it, perfectionism is the enemy of creativity, productivity, and sometimes, sanity! As a creative, I tackled this adversary on a regular basis until I slowly began to fight back. I realized that my pursuit to perfection was a race to nowhere!

In my perfectionistic days, I gave myself such a hard time to be accepted by others, and even myself. I knew on a deeper level that I am smart and hardworking. Working hard with self-compassion is going to allow growth and progression in life. A sweet balance of hard work and gentleness needs to be mastered. Where mistakes drive us towards problem solving and triumphs allow for rejoicing. Being hard on yourself is harsh and painful, no matter how much success you acquire. This harshness is ego-driven and not aligned with your soul, which desires peace.

I needed to validate where this pattern came from, heal through some limiting self-beliefs and understand that there was no need for an external validation, competition, or judgement. I want excellence and I want it for my own growth. I stopped being too hard on myself and made mistakes to allow room for humility and progress. Above all, I learned to forgive myself for my past mistakes in the process.

As a mother, this realization was even more needed. In order to focus on the joyful moments and be mindful, I needed to give myself the permission to take off the superwoman cape. I began to take *imperfect action* unapologetically. As long as I take action in the right direction, I appreciate myself instead of criticizing.

I highly recommend reading the book *The Gifts of Imperfection* by Brené Brown. She talks about this topic beautifully. It was one of the first few books I read when I began personal development work.

In order to create space for growth, grace, and self-compassion, we must give up our perfectionism as it is a self-destructive judgement on ourselves. If my self-worth is attached to being flawless, why would I ever try to learn anything new? After all, learning requires making mistakes.

Ironically, many people pursue perfectionism with the belief that striving for perfection will make them more acceptable to other people and making mistakes is a sign of unintelligence or incompetence. That might be only a survival tactic in childhood if a parent is strictly demanding standardized results.

In adulthood though, what more often happens is that perfectionists are perceived as picky, guarded, or hostile. It pushes people away as you are seen to be intimidating and uptight. You end up putting other people through discomfort in relationships. As you become self-critical and unkind towards yourself, you also become difficult with others around you. Who likes being around highly critical and obsessively compelling people? Believe it or not, when you allow perfectionism to overtake your life, you do become that person!

As I intend to age gracefully, I realize how much each moment matters. I feel like holding on to the beauty of experiences and finding meaning in everything I do. I want to find pleasure and fulfilment of the soul through mindfully soaking in my life events. I want to enjoy successes as well as learn from setbacks with my heart in the right place. I don't want to live for others' approvals and opinions. My higher self is what I seek to uncover through a mindful and *imperfect* journey of acceptance and growth. And there is no room for the petty desires of the ego when you choose to vibrate in higher frequency.

How to Overcome Perfectionism

We must heal and recover from the patterns we adopted in childhood. Everything we need to break unhealthy cycles, is within us. Perfectionism is painful and shows up in unhealthy ways if you don't take control of it. Here are some ways you can overcome it:

- Question your standards. Dismantle your belief in perfectionism. Pursue excellence instead.

- Avoid competing with others. If you have competitive inclinations, journal on this and try to understand why.

- Ignore other people's standards or expectations, which you may have imagined in your mind and may not be fixed. Focus on *your* best effort.

- Allow yourself to make mistakes and learn valuable lessons through them.

- Find coping strategies for overcoming anxiety related to perfectionism. Journal, seek support, exercise, meditate, go on nature walks, explore healing work, talk therapy, or coaching, etc.

- Take imperfect action. Challenge yourself to start working on things without worrying too much about the outcome. Focus on getting things done *well* as opposed to *perfectly*.

- Break your projects into smaller chunks. Divide bigger goals into smaller achievable ones. This will help overcoming procrastination and worrying about the outcome.

- Let your truth be seen. Stop pretending to be someone uncomfortably. Be vulnerable. Share your imperfections without feeling shame. Everyone pretending to be perfect has flaws! Allow authenticity to flow by being yourself. Others will relate to you and connect with you more and you won't feel the pressure to prove yourself to anyone.

Reflect

1. What are some ways perfectionism is affecting your life?
2. What can you do to defeat your perfectionistic habits?
3. Who can help you with this goal?
4. How will overcoming perfectionism help your life?

Whatever is begun in anger, ends in shame.

—Benjamin Franklin

Master Your Emotions

Everything we do in life has a strong emotional component attached to it. On our quest for personal mastery, tuning into our emotions is key. Having self-control means being able to demonstrate appropriate emotions for various situations. When we don't know how to master our emotions, we tend to be in reactive mode to anything that triggers us in some way. Our goal is to become *responsive* to our emotions as we develop *emotional awareness*.

Emotional mastery is the key to personal and professional success. Everyone experiences emotions, which are an essential part of life. However, problems arise when our emotions begin to rule our presence. When our productivity, relationships, and overall experience begins to suffer as a result of emotional overload and mismanagement. The lack of insight into our emotions, i.e., where they originate from and how they shape us, has negative effects on our ability to live our best lives.

Understanding Emotions

Most people like to believe that emotions happen to us. It's because of the weather, the time, the situations, the boss, the spouse, or whatever is outside of yourself, that you want to blame for how you feel. However, the truth is that you can *create* your emotions. They originate from inside of you, giving you more autonomy over them. As you bring more awareness towards your emotional patterns and what triggers them, you begin to slowly shift things around to make your emotions work *for* you and not *against* you.

Emotions play a very important role in our overall experiences. We can rejoice in fully experiencing our positive emotions and not taking them for granted. We can also allow ourselves to feel our difficult emotions and understand why we feel them and not attach any guilt, shame, or negativity for having such feelings. We want to learn what our emotions mean. There are hidden clues and messages within our emotions that require our attention. And it is very important for us to discover all that without feeling any shame or self-judgement. A positive emotion calls for showing intentional gratitude and a negative emotion calls for an introspective response. Emotions sometimes hit us unexpectedly and other times, we create them.

Let's take a basic example to understand how we can create our emotions. Sunshine makes me happy. And I always feel down when the weather is gloomy. It is fine to feel down every now and then. But if it turns into a darker place that impacts me negatively, I must manage it. I know that is my chance to practice *reframing* how I feel. Rainy, gloomy weather could feel depressing and limiting or positive, such as a chance to bake with the family or some personal care time while your car gets washed, and your yard get watered. In Islamic tradition, rain symbolizes blessing, and it is a good time to supplicate. Reframing your experience positively will allow similar emotions to follow. You can create a narrative that makes a rainy day a bad thing or something good you've been waiting for. It's not the events that cause our emotions, but the meanings we tend to attach to our experiences. As you learn to change the meaning, you change your experience.

We may experience more challenging emotions than our day-to-day lows, such as hurt, fear, anger, regret, shame, rejection, etc. We can consciously bring awareness to our negative emotions to really tune in and understand where they originate from and how we can redirect them in healthy ways.

It is not wise to let difficult emotions bottle up inside of us. We must express them and process them. Becoming curious about our emotions can help gain an understanding of who we are and what we need at any point. Asking honest and creative questions can radically change how you emotionally feel about anything.

Some things may be intense for us to go through, such as grief or betrayal. Understand that in your most difficult times, it is important to give yourself grace and time as you allow yourself you go through your emotions, fully validating how challenging it may be.

A mistake a lot of people make is ignoring and distracting themselves from feeling emotional pain. A wholesome human experience invites compassion into our most difficult times so we can come out stronger through our adversities and understand that the emotion is here to guide us towards what's needed. Is it a break? Is it rest? Do we need to talk to someone? Do we need to connect with God? Do we need to be seen and heard? Do we need to pause, meditate, and reflect? What do we need?

The Subconscious Triggers

In *Awaken the Giant Within*, Tony Robbins shares that in order to master your life, you need to master your emotions. He also emphasizes that the *only reason* why anyone does anything is to change the way they feel. Next time you do anything, notice why you do it. (Robbins 1991)

From our daily self-care routines to our work, family life, and social interactions, we are constantly catering to our emotions. Most our emotions are our responses to our life-long programed patterns that are embedded in our subconscious mind and operate on autopilot mode.

Our *subconscious mind* is the root of all emotional triggers. It is important to gain understanding of our triggers and re-program certain things in our minds, allowing us to take control of ourselves. We are all emotional beings; however, everyone processes things differently. Some of us are more sensitive than others. You may feel things way more than your logical/thinker counterparts. That said, those who don't show emotions as much, still feel them and express them in unique ways.

Understanding our distinctive emotional inclinations is important in order to keep ourselves in check. Otherwise, we are just reacting, and the more we react, the more we lose control. The more we lose control, the more we rub off our negative emotional energy onto those around us, presenting a real test for them.

I must confess, as a highly sensitive *feeler* by nature, I get triggered easily. More inner work opportunities for me! It takes a good conscious effort on my part to intentionally choose to frame myself with the right mindset before heading into a new situation. It is a good idea to be neutral and curious in new settings or when reintroducing yourself to any setting after a break.

Typically, situations like family reunions and "going back home" are when we experience big emotional triggers. Perhaps our chances of being misunderstood increase when we are reintroduced to each other with our evolved versions at a different stage in life after a gap. Anything can be perceived as an attack when we feel misunderstood or invalidated after we have changed. This phenomenon made sense to me when I began to explore the *inner child*.

When in childhood, we are taught to distract from emotions and numb them. We are not essentially educated on how to express emotions, process, and release them without shame or guilt. Emotions are known to be "too much." And when we don't get to deal with emotions early on in life, we develop coping mechanisms and behaviours to adapt. These behaviours become our reactive patterns and autopilot responses. Such patterns can be unlearned by connecting with our inner child and beginning to heal our wounds, big or small. Yet, when we return to face those who instigated difficult emotions, invalidated our feelings, or dismissed our self-worth in any way, we are triggered repeatedly.

As we heal, we grow and work towards attaining emotional mastery. But healing is not a linear experience. You will feel like you're ready, aware, grown, and wise, and then boom! It hits you again with some trigger from your past. And you must gain control over it again.

There are many things that began to come up for me in my thirties regarding my *inner child*, which I was completely unaware of for years into my adulthood. As I became more aware of my triggers, I explored deeper within and began to gain an understanding of why I picked up certain patterns, such as perfectionism and people pleasing, and what needed healing. This is not only true for me; it is mostly the case for anyone who developed a self-sabotaging pattern in life.

It is quite mind-blowing how our brains store information. The way we perceive things as a child and how we hold on to certain beliefs well into adulthood. Who you become on an emotional level depends on everything: your personality, your birth order, your parents' mindsets, your life experiences, and who you believe you are as an adult subconsciously. Understanding your triggers can really help to respond to your difficult emotions conscientiously.

The Emotional Triad

Even if we don't choose to go much deeper, it is important to understand our constant state of emotions. What is our regular emotional health and how can we shift it for the better? There are three factors that determine how you feel emotionally. Becoming aware of these can help transform your emotional state. According to the online article "Discover Your Peak State," Tony Robbins, and many psychologists, call it the "emotional triad:" your physiology, focus, and language. (Robbins, Tony Robbins n.d.) Let's go into some detail on these things.

Firstly, your *physiology* plays a big part in how you feel. Every emotion you experience is first felt in your body. If you want to feel more confident, you stand tall, breathe fully, and speak loud and clear. In the same way, if you feel dejected, it matters if you're slumping over, looking down, breathing shallowly, frowning, and speaking quietly. The way you use your body biochemically changes how you feel. I read somewhere that *emotion is created by motion.* Carry a smile, have a great posture, exercise, and watch your emotions follow with confidence.

Practice creates a habitual pattern. When I'm in a tough spot, I take a deep breath and remind myself that I can control my emotions. The more assertive and deeper my voice, the calmer I feel. An incident comes to mind. When she was seven, my youngest girl accidentally burnt our couch by catching fire on a tissue from a nearby lit candle. My collected and calm response towards the very stressful situation made all the difference. I decided to take a deep breath, realizing quickly that the damage would not be undone if I overreacted or panicked, and I gave my little girl, who was quite terrified and saddened by the accident, a tight, loving hug. A few years ago, yeah . . . that was not like me at all! I would react with all my emotions on autopilot mode, creating a traumatic childhood memory for her. Awareness of our physiology in the few seconds that follow any incident can offer a huge emotional advantage.

Secondly, whatever you *focus* on, you feel. If you focus on great things in life, you'll have emotions aligned with that focus. Focus on what could go right and why you can be grateful, and you'll be in a state of positivity. Similarly, when you feel depressed, your focus is not on all the good in life, you ignore the good and zero in on the negative and magnify it. If you are reminded of a negative experience from the past, you feel the negative emotions you felt back then and relive that depressing state of emotion again. In doing so, you begin to overthink and create disruption in your present experience.

We must train our minds to shift our focus quickly to not allow our minds to wander in any direction that might bring our emotions down. What's bad is always available to you, and so is what's good; what you choose to access and focus on grows. In any moment, you can shift your focus towards something good.

And lastly, your *language* patterns also impact your emotional experience tremendously. If you say things like, I feel really exhausted, or, This is too hard, or Why me? you will literally feel those emotions. Such words don't put you in an empowering state. You feel like making excuses and playing victim. Your words have different emotional states associated to them. Being aware of your vocabulary and statements in your speech make you conscious of how you feel. Begin to say things like, I can do this, I'll figure it out, This phase won't last, or Let me take a moment and process this, and you'll begin to condition yourself for confidence and calmness. Affirm to yourself all the things you want to manifest, and your emotions will follow.

We are always practicing some form of self-talk on a subconscious level. Most of the times we don't even realize and begin to verbalize things that we are accustomed to *believing* about ourselves deep inside. Bring some awareness to what your inner talk looks like. What are some of the things you believe inside that bring you down? You'll notice that a lot of the proof of your emotional state lies in your speech patterns. As you bring awareness to your language, you can begin to shift positively and feel accordingly.

The truth is, you can feel any emotion you want by *deciding* to feel it. Happiness is a choice and so is sadness, anger, frustration, or any other emotion. Here's a truth bomb: no one makes you feel *happy* or *sad*. How you feel is based on how you're interpreting each situation in your life and the meaning you associate to it. That is not to say that difficult emotions are not allowed. Awareness of why we feel them and how we can process and pass through tough emotions is important. When you learn to take charge of how you feel, everything shifts in your life. Anyone can be trained on this skill.

> *I don't want to be at the mercy of my emotions. I want to use*
> *them, to enjoy them, and to dominate them.*
> —Oscar Wilde

Emotional Intelligence

Also known as the emotional quotient (EQ), emotional intelligence (EI) refers to the ability to perceive, control, and respond to one's emotions as well as others. Some suggest that emotional intelligence can be learned and strengthened, while others claim it's an inborn characteristic. The ability to express and manage emotions is essential, but so is the ability to understand and respond to the emotions of others with empathy. Psychologists refer to this ability as emotional intelligence, and some experts even suggest that it can be more important than your IQ for overall success in life. I agree with that. Human connection is empty without emotional intelligence. Most people are drawn to those who listen, connect, and hold space for others' emotions.

How does EI manifest in your daily interactions? Being able to accept criticism and be responsible. Moving on after making a mistake. Knowing how to share your feelings with others. Being able to solve problems in ways that work for all parties. Having empathy for other people. Having great listening skills. Not being judgemental of others or jumping to conclusions. Being open minded to hear different ideas and perspectives. These are all manifestations of high emotional intelligence.

Having emotional intelligence doesn't mean you don't have difficulty with your emotions. One may have an occasional outburst upon being triggered, only to process everything and arrive at a stable place afterwards. Only after having your reactive hurtful moments, and becoming aware of them, will you learn to invite responsiveness, pause, and control when emotionally triggered. Just like anything else in life, this takes time and practice.

Emotional intelligence is essential for good interpersonal connections. Understanding emotions can be the key to better relationships, improved well-being, and stronger communication skills. People who have fewer emotional skills tend to get into more arguments, have lower quality relationships, and have poor emotional coping skills.

When communicating, keep in mind, which hat you wear in the context of the message you share. Who you are in relation to the receiver and how you must articulate your message accordingly is a very necessary skill to develop. Be confident, self-assured, yet humble. Humility and confidence co-exist in a highly charismatic individual, inviting the receiver in and allowing them to be vulnerable and authentic with you. Don't we all want such connections? We yearn for them. But very few people understand that they require skills.

Growing your EI will also help develop emotional mastery within yourself. To improve your EI, work on becoming a good listener, speak slowly and intentionally, empathize with others, compliment others genuinely, and reflect on the outcomes of your emotions. Understanding why people behave the way they do and noticing how others trigger emotions within you can be a sign of improved emotional intelligence. As you grow your EI, you'll notice a positive change in your overall emotional well-being.

How to Develop Emotional Mastery

Like any skill, emotional mastery can be developed with effort and practice. Get out your journal when you want to sort through difficult emotions and write things down. Here are a few steps I share with my clients when dealing with difficult emotions:

1. *Identify and bring awareness.* You can't change what you're not aware of. Bring awareness to how your emotions play out. What situations, events, or words trigger you? What do you feel in the moment? Label your emotion, such as, "I feel anxious or overwhelmed." Notice how you behave when you're triggered. Are you minimizing or exaggerating your behaviour? What is the impact of your reaction on yourself and others?

2. *Understand and accept.* Know that feeling negative emotions is not *bad*. Eliminate your resistance towards your emotions and try to understand them. Get curious about the hints your emotions present to you. Your emotions provide data to allow honest conversations within yourself. This data is helpful in processing emotions to become more resilient and aware.

3. *Choose to respond consciously.* Try to take a neutral stance. Once you interrupt your current emotional pattern, you can think through your options and brainstorm about how to prevent your emotions to overwhelm you or control you. Seek help if this is difficult to do on your own. You always have the power to respond to your emotions mindfully.

4. *Think of the big picture.* If something is not going to matter in a few days or weeks, don't bother yourself much. Allow emotions to flow easily instead of holding on for too long. Zoom out and take a good look at the true impact of whatever you are feeling. Don't give a home to a difficult emotion within yourself for too long. Once the emotion has done its job, move on.

We feel many kinds of emotions in each day. It is when we allow our negative emotions to overwhelm us and overtake us, that they become problematic. Emotional mastery requires awareness and intentional reprograming. Program yourself to become a problem solver. Transform your helplessness into empowerment by bringing your actions in alignment with how you want to feel. This approach gets you unstuck and helps you move forward with confidence. Remember that you have the potential to overcome anything you want. As you tell yourself a more powerful story, you rewire yourself to show up emotionally strong.

Reflect

1. Think about your constant emotional state on a daily basis. Is it generally positive or negative?

2. Label your challenging emotions.

3. Which negative emotion/s will you begin to process and shift?

4. What do you need to process your difficult emotions? (ex. Coaching, Therapy, journaling etc.)

5. In what ways can you grow your EI?

If you can imagine it, you can achieve it. If you can dream it, you can become it.

—William Arthur Ward

Dream

I wish growing up as a child, instead of pushing down a few options of professions to pursue in life, we were allowed to dream freely. Exploring different interests at a young age is of significant value. I wish dreams were taken more seriously and supported strongly. This itself could build our self-esteems and give us the chance to take on opportunities earlier in life without limitations of customary standards.

Many of us are asked this question in childhood, "What do you want to be when you grow up?" We may not always know the answer. Sometimes this question instills some anxiety within us. The reason is that society programs us to this idea that there's one thing we must be when we grow up and devote our life to it. It is what becomes your title, your profession, your purpose and you may identify with that more than anything else. The idea pressurizes us through college, and we struggle to prove ourselves and are scared to change our direction. Many of us are not wired this way. We have a lot of passions and things we may want to pursue. If you can relate to that, there is no room for you in the typical framework. You have potential to have multiple passions and many creative pursuits. You get to dream!

The question we need to be asked throughout our younger years should be, "What are your dreams?" or even "What will you dream?" This makes things personal, and one can passionately pursue different dreams. At any stage in life, you can dream of a new dream.

Everyone is born with unique gifts to offer in this world. These can be our dreams that appear often based on our strengths and passions. We can make them known and create an immense impact through dreaming big. However, by the time we are adults, most people get so caught up in their conventional lifestyles that they either get distracted and forget their dreams, keep them hidden deep inside, or shrink them in their minds. Whether these dreams come true or not, it is crucial to keep on dreaming and visualizing in our minds. What's possible for us cannot be revealed unless we first imagine it to be.

Most of us make our life choices based on expectations. We go to college, get married, have children, and settle down, because that's what everyone does. We forget that we also have dreams for ourselves. Things we desire to do, plans we make for our lives based on our individual values, our longing for doing interesting things, experiencing, exploring, and becoming masterful. Everyone has dreams within them. If pursued with eagerness and grit, one can achieve anything.

What Are Dreams?

Dreams are your intrinsic aspirations, ideas, or goals that you cherish in your heart or develop over time. Dreaming is about designing your life based on who you are as a unique individual. Ask yourself these questions:

- What kind of life do you want to live?
- What lifestyle choices do you wish to make?
- What is fulfilling for you?
- What is your ideal version of yourself and your family?
- What do you want to learn and achieve?
- What talents do you already have within you naturally that you want to improve?
- Which new skills do you desire to acquire?
- What change are you passionate to bring about in your family/ community/world?

See, a dream is not only there to plan your future career, as we are told from a young age. Rather, it is also about discovering and believing in yourself to create what's possible for you in different ways. Dreams can be big or small. Your dream is never invalid. The times you catch yourself say something like, I wish I could . . . or, I really want to do . . . those are your moments to catch yourself and hold on to that thought or idea a little bit longer.

Don't just think about it and discard the thought later. Make it valid and tangible by writing it down, sharing it with someone, and imagining how actually being able to fulfill your dream would feel like. Dreaming opens a whole world of imagination and possibility. Once you allow yourself to dream, you can set and achieve goals much easier. When you see possibility, you begin to plan and act upon what you believe is attainable.

Why Dream?

Your dreams can be passion driven or purpose driven. Whether intrinsic or extrinsic in nature, a dream gives us a sense of direction. It enables us to envision what may be possible aside from the mundane life. Where *passion* is for your own fulfilment, *purpose* has a bigger meaning. It is your ideal for what you wish to acquire on a soulful level or for what you give to others. When led by purpose, one contributes from a deeper, more meaningful place. You change the world in your own little way. You are driven to solve a problem or help others in a way you are gifted and capable of. When you begin to believe that you are chosen for a certain kind of impact in the world, big or small, you show up differently.

Our dreams keep us motivated and inspire us to explore new ideas. We already have our intrinsic inspirations and inclinations that are unique to us. Our job is to bring them to the surface. If we ignore our need to dream, we can't set an intention to achieve anything greater than what is considered basic. We live in a system that makes us believe that staying comfortable inside the box is easy and dreams are for those who rebel and are willing to leave the comfort zones. In my humble opinion, dreaming is where it all begins, and it is for everyone.

Your dreams and goals can help you make life choices and engage in certain behaviours that can put you on the path toward achieving your aspirations. Aspirations also offer a glimpse into the type of life you might hope for in the future. Having a vision for the future helps you to stay focused on the things that you need to do to ultimately make your dream happen.

Most people struggle with their self-esteem, at one point in time or another. The truth of the matter is, people who keep setting goals for themselves and explore possibilities feel more accomplished and develop higher self-esteems. Anything you ever want can come true. So really, the question is: What do you believe in? If your belief in yourself and what's possible for your life is limited, then you must dig deeper and find out why. Set new intentions in order to change your limiting belief system as you dare to dream.

Put a certain amount of work towards a simple dream such as learning a new skill. Stay consistent and keep track of your progress. You'll notice a shift in how confident you feel in pursuing your dream.

Why Most People Don't Dream

We all have dreams deep down within us. But we seldom recognize them or believe in our potentials to pursue them. There are two possible outcomes of having dreams. One is for the few self-aware people who learn to recognize their inner longings as significant and devote their time and energy to nourishing those desires. These people see possibility in achieving their dreams.

The second outcome is for those who have self-doubt and are reluctant to act upon their inner callings. They simply don't do anything about it. They are scared to take the path seldom travelled. For these types, their dream becomes "just a dream." So, if you are the later type, we just need some inner work to bring about the necessary shift towards living your ideal life that you dream of.

Most people don't dream because they assume that you must be a certain kind of person to dare to do things that ordinary people don't do. If you ask me, we are all extraordinary. We just believe otherwise! You have dreams inside of you that are just not acknowledged by you 'yet'. Once you begin to recognize what you're capable of, your subconscious belief system will shift, new pathways will come into sight, and actions will follow.

We are naturally wired to protect ourselves and play safe. So, whenever we think of anything new or big that seems impossible at the moment, our instincts tell us, Well that's not going to happen, or, This will be so hard for me so why bother? Guest what? That is exactly the kind of mindset you need to stay stagnant and boring and unsuccessful and unconfident in life! The good news is we can overcome our preprogramed conditioning and old thinking habits that hinder our growth.

Many of us are unable to dream and pursue our passions because of our inner beliefs about what we *should* work on. Here I would like to mention a bitter truth. We grow up with the biggest lie that robs us of our confidence in life. We are told by parents, teachers, and other authority figures that if we are not good at something, then we must do more of that, and become better. This technique works for learning life skills and things like driving practice, but certainly not for math or history or sports if we lack the interest altogether. We can't force ourselves to draw more if we hate to draw, yet if we enjoy it, we will excel by practicing more.

Similarly, a certain career cannot be imposed upon an individual. By focusing on your weaknesses, you end up feeling inferior subconsciously. We should teach to get amazing at what we're already interested in or are naturally good at. If we don't know what that is 'yet', well then keep exploring and practicing different things. Soon enough, you'll know! Dreams can easily become a true reality if they are aligned with what you already love doing, as opposed to what you were taught to compete with. If your cousin became a doctor, it doesn't mean you have to also follow the same path to be known as *successful*. Define your own success through pursuing your unique dream.

People think they are too old to dream. It is never too late to dream. In fact, there is no age or timeline for any kind of personal development. Don't let anyone make you think like it's too late to dream and set new goals. Think, What makes me happy and fulfilled? What do I want to achieve? What will that require? Imagine, visualize, plan.

Build the Courage

Many people are so worried about falling short or failing that they dump their dreams altogether. They avoid taking on exciting risks or entertaining new opportunities just because of the fear of failure. Our fears can have a strange hold on us. They keep us small and unhappy. If we give *failure* a new meaning, we can build the courage to dream.

If you have the fear of rejection, judgement, or disappointment keeping you back, you need to overcome these blocks to step outside of your ego-led inner critic, who is always at war with your dreams. There might be a version of the same old *I'm-not-good-enough* story playing in the back of your mind.

A lot of people know they are passionate and talented, but they underestimate their potential to be able to make their difference. That is where we need a little more courage. It always seems too big at first to dream about anything bigger than ourselves. But as we begin to visualize and imagine possibilities, things begin to line up accordingly. It is a mind's game really!

I always knew I wanted to write a book in my life. It was one of my dreams. I remember thinking to myself, I'll write my book when I turn fifty and my nest is empty, as then I will have more time. The best lesson I learned from my mentors is that I only have the present moment. If I want to do something, I must believe that it is possible and there is something I can do about it today. I stayed inspired by following successful examples and implemented some new disciplines to become an author. I decided to get started when I was thirty-nine. I worked at my slow pace, made mistakes, procrastinated, took imperfect action, and here I am!

Most people are shy and scared to share their dreams with others. Well, if you keep your dreams and aspirations to yourselves, they will never materialize, will they? By sharing your dreams with (trustworthy) others, you build the needed pressure and accountability. Your dreams stay hidden if you don't have them known. Build the courage to dream and talk about your dreams as if you are convinced that they will materialize.

Finding other like-minded people wanting to achieve similar goals as you, can be helpful in staying motivated. Setting new goals takes courage and accomplishing them takes a lot of energy and discipline. How you live your present brings you closer to your desired future. One must begin to talk about it before they gain the courage to work towards their dream.

If you talk about it, it's a dream. If you envision it, it's possible. If your schedule it, it's real.
—Tony Robbins

How to Dream

Think of what feels rewarding to you. What brings joy for you and upgrades your life? Explore the things that you love doing or feel strongly about or wish to accomplish. It could be anything physical, spiritual, inspirational, educational, professional, artistic, etc. Maybe there is a legacy you wish to leave behind.

Here are some questions to ask yourself: how can I give from my gifts, time, knowledge, or energy? Who can I learn more from to improve? What is it that I already do well? What is something others can learn from me? That's basically the train of thought you can follow.

Start thinking on a personal level first. Your unique life story has inspiration hidden inside it. Perhaps something you learned and mastered in your life can become a bigger purpose. What do you want to change within yourself or your situation? Perhaps you achieve a fitness goal or a relationship goal. You might end up achieving a goal that inspires you to change others' lives in meaningful ways. You may dream to provide a certain lifestyle for your family. And as you succeed through your struggles, you may have a powerful story to share with others who wish the same.

Think about how fascinating it would be to make your own little difference in the world? A sincere intention can take you very close to taking action. Just saying it out loud can make it real in your mind. Here are some ideas for you to journal about to find and pursue your dreams:

- Make a list of things you are passionate about or ways you are talented.
- Think of things that fill you with joy or ways you want to contribute.
- What are your goals for yourself in the future? Any improvements or changes you wish to make.
- Express your dream to someone reliable who can hold you accountable to make it a reality.
- Create a plan to achieve your dream. Think about what you would need to learn, who you need to meet/connect with, what needs to change in your life to get you closer to your dreams.

Reflect

1. Write down your most important dream for yourself.
2. What can you do as your small action steps towards achieving your dream?
3. How will you feel and how will your life change if you could fulfil your dream?
4. How can you dream more and set goals for yourself?

You can choose courage or you can choose comfort. You cannot have both.

—Brené Brown

Expand Your Comfort Zone

Most people consider their comfort zone to be where they feel *safe* in life. It could be a place you have been used to for a long time. But your comfort zone can also indicate your fears, limitations, progress, and quality of life. The choices you make based on comfort are very different than the ones you make for excellence, growth, and achievement. An exceptional mindset is required for up levelling your life experience that pushes your boundaries and expands your potential.

From a psychological standpoint, your comfort zone is an artificial mental boundary within which you maintain a sense of security and out of which you experience discomfort. It is a safe bubble which is customary but not necessarily blissful. People tend to stay within their comfort zones just to be comfortable. In doing so, they also remain stagnant and restrict their ability to enhance their lives. They stay away from the unknowns and avoid difficulty or hard work. But the reality is, people don't realize how limiting their own comfort zones are.

People who are rigid in their ways and avoid change, can lack self-confidence when put in new situations. If we stay within our comfort zones, we lack trusting our abilities. Confidence is built on trusting one's abilities and skills. If we are hesitant to grow our abilities, we will lack confidence.

Your "Zone" Defines You

Your comfort zone reflects your limits and how you think and expect things should be. Your ability to change yourself or your situation also depends on how *comfortable* you choose to be. If you're willing to

173

challenge yourself and escape what's known to you, you develop a new belief that: overcoming, exploring, healing, fixing, trying, or changing for the better are all possible and within your reach.

What choices you make in your life depend on your zone. Are you going to expand beyond your current known patterns, or will you fold up into routines and fixed beliefs? Are you going to recreate yourselves repeatedly or settle and compromise? Most people choose to sink into familiar roles, old stories, and viewpoints and are scared to expand and explore anything new, uncustomary, or challenging.

When you are in a challenging situation, or one that doesn't fit your expectations, you usually do whatever you can to make yourself comfortable again. For many people, even if they are unhappy or unfulfilled, their natural inclination is to stay within the comfort zone simply because it is familiar and supposedly safe. Many people stay in jobs, relationships, habitual patterns, and situations that don't serve them any longer. However, they stick to them just because they are afraid of the unknown or they are not prepared to face change.

The truth is that security lies within us due to habitual thinking and feeling patterns we acquire over time. These patterns become our program that runs on autopilot mode within us. It is what we have found comfort in, whether it serves us or not. We convince ourselves that it is our reality and consider anything new to be risky or difficult. This mindset must be questioned and challenged in order to escape any situation that doesn't serve our growth and fulfilment.

Our daily habits make up who we become. Things like sleeping in, overeating, wasting time, watching TV for hours, addiction to the phone, inactivity, saying negative things, doubting people's intentions, holding grudges, etc. Now these things can have a massive effect on our way of becoming if we don't intentionally challenge ourselves. These are all examples of habits or behaviours that harm us, and we must learn to change them instead of staying too comfortable in them.

To give another example, being overweight and out of shape can become comfortable to someone, making them unhappy and powerless. They may believe that they will never lose weight as they become too comfortable with the supposition such a desirable change is inaccessible to them or requires an impossible amount of work, which is outside of their comfort zone. To change their situation, they must be willing to let go of their lifestyle, whether it is laziness, overeating, lack of physical fitness, or a way of thinking that doesn't serve them. Unless they decide to become self-disciplined about some things in their life and take action, they won't escape their comfort zone, which is keeping them miserable.

Similarly, staying in a *victim mindset* can be comfortable for someone because that is all they have been used to. However, for someone who has overcome that mindset and is functioning in *creative mode*, playing victim will become highly uncomfortable. Such a person has now chosen to escape the comfort zone, where they were accustomed to making up self-sabotaging stories that kept them unhappy and powerless. Now, they may be uncomfortable there and have expanded into feeling more limitless, abundant, and empowered.

So, comfort zones vary from person to person and define people differently based on their individual *zones*. It does require the courageous act of confronting oneself to escape one's comfort zone. I don't suggest you leave what's known and comfortable to you abruptly. Instead, work on expanding it little by little. Unfortunately, if you choose to remain in your comfort zone, you will not know what your true potential is. By expanding your comfort zone, you begin to discover what you are capable of achieving. What your comfort zone allows becomes your reality. Whether it's your thoughts, feelings, habits, behaviours, self-image, career opportunities, skill sets, life exposure, relationships—you name it! Everything remains the same in a comfort zone, and you become a hostage to it if you choose to stay in it.

What's Keeping You Stuck?

Many people will stay where they are in life because they think that either the time is not right, or they are not ready. Trust me, you will never be ready for something new if you fear the outcome or worry about being prepared enough. It's never going to feel like the right time. The time is *now*! There are no limitations of age, time, or ability once you firmly decide to change something for the better.

When people convince themselves that they "can't" do something or they are "not good at" something, they are stuck in a *fixed mindset*. They are accustomed to believing what's possible for them based on their easy known ways. But if you were to ask anyone if they want to grow, achieve, and become better and do things they admire others doing, they will not hesitate to say "yes!"

Most people are stuck in their ways because they are unaware that they are stuck. It is important to bring awareness to the fact that *staying too comfortable* is a problem. With this awareness, you'll be able to point out where it is that you need to expand your comfort zone. Regardless of what needs to change, I can assure you that it begins in your mind. With a newly acquired belief in possibility and potential, you can shift pretty much anything in life. But first you need to allow yourself to accept becoming uncomfortable enough to bring about your desired outcomes.

If you want positive change in life, you need to challenge yourself. There is an old saying that defines *insanity* as the *expectation that acting in the same way will produce different results.* Most people want better results in life. However, very few are willing to do anything differently. People who are successful and happy have mastered the *art of change*. They are not afraid to revisit their prior actions and approach things differently. They courageously expand their comfort zones for growth to occur.

You must not want to remain stagnant in life—mentally, physically, spiritually, professionally, in relationships, etc. For you to grow as a person, you must be unhappy with redundancy. Humans are seekers of growth and development by nature. We want to use our intelligence in new ways. We desire excitement, inspiration, accomplishment, and confidence. All these things make us happy. Holding on to same old repetitive lifestyle within our comfort zones can be boring. Self-confidence is built upon accomplishing new goals as we push our limits and escape our comfort zones. If you don't move forward in anyway, you end up staying the same and stop growing, which is actually moving you backwards.

What's Outside Your Comfort Zone?

Growth and success lie outside the comfort of your safety net. The people, habits, systems, lifestyle, or whatever is keeping you limited, can be challenged and changed for the better. Unless you are courageous enough to venture out of the comfort zone, you won't see new possibilities or seek higher potential. If, however, you make the decision to move beyond the circumstances, people, and experiences you are familiar with, you move out of your comfort zone and onto the path of personal development. This is where it gets exciting! This path forces you to stretch yourself, push your limits, and become more than you previously were. This is the new zone, also called your *growth zone.*

Take it slow! This new unfamiliar zone can also be your *panic zone* as it may induce fear, worry, or trigger things inside you that you never experienced before. That is all part of the package. Slowly but surely, you'll taste the fruits in this new zone. As you allow change and see results, you will be compelled to continuously grow your capacity for achieving.

Just like previously I thought, because of my one weak arm, injured hip, my age, and others convincing me that it was a bad idea, I couldn't do advanced balance poses on my head! I had to decide for myself to trust my ability and give it a chance. I practiced, failed many times, pushed myself bit by bit, and now I can do head stands and a few variations of balance poses I never thought I could imagine before. I expanded my capacity by becoming uncomfortable and challenging myself. The work comes before your see any results. Trust yourself to take the leap. Growth feels way better than comfort in my opinion. And comfort never builds confidence!

> *Growth and comfort can't ride the same horse.*
> —*Margie Warrell*

With proper awareness towards our fears and possible anxiety related to escaping the comfort zones, we can explore taking baby steps. Break down your anxiety into incremental growth. If you're struggling with losing certain amount of weight, don't overwhelm yourself with the big picture. Just start by planning next week's gym visits and take on mini challenges. Soon enough, you'll become accustomed to facing you fears and pushing through to gain ideal results.

The customary norms and ideologies may keep us stuck inside our comfort zones. Doing what others do, not questioning other options or possibilities, and relying on what's popular can be limiting for many people. Human intelligence is far advanced than just going with the norm. If one is inspired to explore new ways, one must build the courage to look outside the box. Well, firstly, begin to question the box! Why does it even have to exist?

For example, for homeschooling our children, in the beginning, there was a lot of anticipation and negativity we had to deal with. We had very little support from others, and many were doubtful of our choices. It was certainly something which required our family to go way outside of our comfort zones to explore new possibilities, ideas, and experiences. Against all odds, we went against the flow and created an enriching lifestyle that suited the vision for our family. Through questioning what was customary and common, we found new possibilities. In this way, we discovered many benefits of pursuing our unique path that could only exist outside of the comfort zone.

Benefits of Expanding Your Comfort Zone

As your mind opens to new possibilities, you begin to find joy in new experiences. You may try new recipes, meet different people, explore new places, and travel. Here are some added benefits you can enjoy when you aim to grow your comfort zone:

- You attempt to learn new skills and grow possibilities.
- You become open to picking up new hobbies, regardless of your age.
- You feel younger and high-spirited.
- You access your creativity and try different approaches in life.
- It shifts your perspectives and enables you to overcome your limitations.
- It can prevent boredom and enhance your mental health.

- Your self-confidence increases and you become more resilient and self-assured.
- You become more relatable and accessible for others, which improves relationships.
- It increases your overall happiness index and make you more interesting.

Over the past few years, I've learned that if I expect better results from my life in any way, I can look at my current habitual patterns and begin to challenge them. The magic lies outside of my comfort zone. It allows me to dare and try new things. Taking new challenges and setting new goals is easier for me now. Trusting my previous experience, relying on my instincts, and using my limited wisdom is all I need to take my next leap!

Challenging Yourself

Begin with subtle ways to challenge yourself like taking a new course or lesson, trying new recipes, trying out a new service (like getting your first massage or going for therapy), learning a new language or skill, taking up a new sport, starting a new project, or building a new habit. Reach out to new people and network with them.

Break from a routine or habit you've had for a long time and replace it with a better one. If you're typically an inactive person, find a physical activity you can enjoy. Or if you're normally very active, take breaks to wind down and relax, challenge yourself to read or meditate.

Go to an ethnic restaurant and try dishes from a different culture. It will stimulate your taste buds and open you to a whole new cuisine. Perhaps challenge yourself to cook new foods using different ingredients at home as well. These small efforts will open you to the possibility of changing and evolving.

Look at your life with this new perspective of thinking of ways to challenge yourself.

- How can you add fresh perspectives to your life?
- In what ways can you be more open-minded?

- What patterns have you repeated for a very long time that could be broken with a different outlook?
- What new actions can be introduced in your lifestyle?
- What new habit can you build?
- What is too redundant and unsatisfactory in your life that needs to be spiced up?

You will learn that the more you push yourself to expand your comfort zone, little by little, the more you will begin to enjoy new things and take risks, which might lead to new possibilities that spark joy.

> *The journey of a thousand miles begins with a single step.*
> —*Lao Tzu*

Travel

One of many ways to grow your comfort zone is to travel to new places. If you've lived your whole life seeing the world from your front yard, you're missing out—big time! One sure way to stay open-minded and broaden your perspectives, is to travel. It makes you a more interesting, insightful, and relatable as a person. It expands you, enlightens you, and teaches you about the variety of people, lifestyles, and cultures. It is a pursuit well worth saving for. Don't rely on the news to get educated on different cultures and lifestyles. Read, search, and travel yourself to form your own opinions and judgements based on raw experiences.

I've met many people from different backgrounds through my business. The most open-minded are those who have travelled and explored more than the ordinary Canadian. A recent visit to Turkey for myself was an exceptional experience that grew our family in exciting new ways. It was such a breath of fresh air after two years of constant COVID-restricted narratives surrounding us. It felt like an escape and allowed us to notice how differently another nation handles a pandemic. Observing a new culture broadened our perspectives and taught us different things, which opened many interesting conversations in our household.

Traveling is so important for getting away from your everyday, mundane lifestyle and becoming a stranger in a new land. You feel like an explorer who welcomes adventure and exciting new experiences. Give yourself the gift of becoming a little carefree, a little exotic, a little curious. Treat yourself to some new foods, wear local clothing, talk to new people, and understand perspectives from an unknown land. Go without any preconceived judgements and simply observe. Notice how that evolves you on a personal level.

Start a Business

If you want to expand your comfort zone on many levels, start a small business, a new project, a movement, a book club, a support club, or pursue anything that you might be passionate about. It will teach you many skills like public speaking, leadership, communication, problem solving, how to learn from mistakes, and keep going.

I believe that owning your business can be full of opportunities for growth if you are committed to living a fulfilled life. If this is highly unlikely for you to take on, think about brushing up a skill and becoming an expert at something you love. Anything that fulfils you or helps you to contribute in some way.

My small business allowed ownership of my talent and potential, understanding my limitations, and expanding my comfort zone. For me, it was an amazing opportunity for self-discovery. The more I put myself out there in different situations, I realized how much I needed to learn. I noticed potential for my talent, ideas for collaboration, and the benefits of networking. I learned how to represent myself outside of what I had known my identity to be previously. I became confident with my craft and attracted new opportunities.

An entrepreneurial experience strengthens our habit of looking for our own answers and asserting our preferences. In doing so, we find more deeper aspects of life such as understanding ourselves, knowing our vision, and claiming our potential. Owning your business is a solo path, kind of like homeschooling! It doesn't allow you to back down too quickly. You feel responsible to figure things out for yourself. You research. You try new things. You develop tenacity. You don't give up easily.

I wouldn't have learned how to overcome my fears and step out of my comfort zone if I didn't run a small business. It requires you to build great relationships with people. You get to put yourself out there in the unknown territory. Networking is important for both personal and professional growth. You learn to manage personal life better once you can manage a business. From controlling emotions to time management, you get to evolve as an entrepreneur and in turn, as a person. For many entrepreneurs, the approach to life becomes more wholesome.

Ways to Grow your Comfort Zone

Starting a business or travelling may not be accessible to everyone. You can start by slowly growing your comfort zone regularly. Here are some helpful ideas:

- Challenge your thoughts. Be curious and use what-ifs in your thought process to look at things from different angles.

- Learn a new skill or take a course. For example, join a group like Toastmasters International where they encourage you to speak in public by using helpful techniques.

- Do something you always wanted to try. Perhaps a bucket list item is waiting to be checked off.

- Take on a new physical challenge for yourself. Perhaps fitness, reading, diet related, or habitual. Commit to something new and stay consistent for a time period.

- Do something out of the ordinary. Something you admire others do and never attempted yourself, such as horseback riding or canoeing.

It is easy and familiar to live the basic life you are very capable of. It can be boring and unfulfilling though. Stretching yourself and expanding your comfort zone is an important part of personal development that should not be ignored. It advances you to the next level in life and keeps you on the path of self-transformation as you broaden your horizons.

There is no passion to be found playing small—in settling for a
life that is less than the one you are capable of living.
    —*Nelson Mandela*

Reflect

1. After reading the ideas presented in this chapter, what are some
   ways you can expand your current comfort zone? Make a list.

2. How can expanding your comfort zone change your life?

3. What is one small challenge you can attempt now?

Inspiration, from whatever the source, arouses feelings within us that rekindle hope, ambition, and determination.

—Jim Rohn

Find Your People

How many times have you heard people say, "I don't feel like I belong," or "I feel lonely," or "No one understands what I'm going through," or "People don't value me," or "I don't fit in," etc.? Well, I have been that person many times. I yearned to feel connection in order to enhance my life experiences. If you're a highly passionate individual, you may need to explore deeper connections and seek out your people.

Ask yourself: do I feel like I belong to a community of people? There is a deep sense of safety in being around people whom you can connect with. You feel understood when there is some sort of commonality between you and others. It could be just one thing that you connect on. This awareness of belonging protects one from feeling lonely or being a misfit. A like-minded group can inspire you and make you feel validated, which helps you thrive in your endeavours.

Now, I'm not talking about your childhood friendships that you may not find any commonality with anymore, yet you continue to drag them along your journey just to remain loyal and share your life with. What many people mistakenly do is, they try to force connections with their old relations or friends. They may also try to prove themselves to be accepted by those whom they already know and trust. It scares them to trust others outside of their known "circle" as they never explore outside of it. And sadly, the need to stay within their comfort zones can be very harmful and lonely for them. People normally reject new ideas such as *finding new people*.

Growth Requires New People

When you want to grow as a person, or when you deal with unique situations, a lot shifts within you. Having a like-minded association that serves you on a deeper level is very different from an old friendship or family member that may be expected to know and support you. Knowing what place you give people that exist in your life can be an art to learn. Yet allowing new people in can be a much-needed requirement. A new chapter in life can demand a new influence. A different experience or challenge can necessitate a deeper support system. A life changing inspiration can be pursued easily with adept motivation or mentorship.

We tend to strive too hard to explain ourselves to get our friends' approvals and often stop daring to do new things that are bigger than their imaginations. This urge hinders us from exploring ourselves and fulfilling our dreams. We tend to have false expectations from close relations as we want them to cheer us on with our newer choices in life.

I find it interesting how we outgrow some relationships when we are growing as a person. It becomes harder to explain your aspirations and ideas to those who are stuck in their comfort zones. It is okay if your personal growth calls for dumping some old friends or distancing yourself from relationships that don't understand you or your pursuits. Start by setting stronger boundaries with your people and turning inwards. There is always the right crowd that is ready to cheer you on, relate with you, or provide support. You have to make the effort to find it.

I have spoken to many coaching clients who suffer in silence and never seek out a community or support. My recent client with ADHD, who was yearning to be understood, was surprised to know how much similarity and support is available online for them. Just knowing that you are not struggling alone can make things easier to handle than suffering in silence.

How to Find Your People

Look for like-minded individuals. As you are discovering yourself and trying new things, whether it is for leisure, business, or personal growth, reach out to the people with similar interests. You could try volunteering, taking classes, attending events, going to meet-ups, or joining clubs and groups that you resonate with. Sign up for a workshop to practice a hobby or enhance a skill (arts, photography, cooking, parenting) and connect with others. There are all kinds of book clubs, support groups, writing clubs, and business networking events. Find a community that feels authentic to you and lights you up. Engage in activities that ignite your soul.

It becomes easier to ask creative questions, share knowledge, or be vulnerable when you feel like you belong. Part of belonging is feeling understood. It is a sense of safety with our vulnerabilities. The internet makes that even easier these days and it is sad to see that people are lonelier than ever. They are hiding behind masks, scared to voice their need to belong. Connect with others using whatever medium you are comfortable with. But please, don't keep yourself hidden inside your bubble! It can seem hard, but once you begin asking and reaching out, you'll be surprised how many other like-minded people are out there looking to connect and share with you.

My "Tribes"

I've always been kind of a misfit, an innovator, the trendsetter, who dabbled into atypical ideas. This required for me to find my people to connect with. I have a few small communities that I access and contribute towards. In my specific contacts, I feel understood, connected and seen much more than my own friends and family. Having homeschooled my children for many years, I joined a couple of homeschooling groups for support and activities with other homeschoolers, which helped me overcome the need to be understood by family and friends who didn't always support my unconventional path.

As a small business owner, meeting up and staying connected to the entrepreneurial world is important for me. And as I refine my skills and grow as a life coach, I have joined a few supportive groups of other renowned coaches and motivational speakers to keep me inspired. I also repurposed my social media presence to connect with like-minded individuals who pursue personal growth.

I make soulful connections to have those deep spiritual conversations, whether I find those in the mosque, my henna studio, or at the yoga practice! The point is, you must create the feeling within you that you belong and matter and can make your difference.

If you have exciting ideas, hobbies, dreams, goals, or even the desire to be a better version of yourself in anyway (such as wanting to lose weight or eat healthy), I encourage you to find a community of like-minded individuals instead of looking for advice from family and friends who may not have the necessary know-how. They might advise you only based on their limited knowledge and experience and may not be able to support you if you make choices that don't agree with their own.

Many times, people are trying to protect us through advising us to not take risks and *playing it safe.* Even though people have great intentions, it may keep us stuck. When we don't find approval, validation, or support from those who we think know us well, we feel discouraged to try new things or share our struggles or dreams. So, share them with those who will understand and support you.

Whether it is a strength or a weakness you may have, a great way to find support or help others can be through staying connected to your specific community as you open up to others. And if there is nothing out there for what you are hoping to find, start your own.

Support Groups

Finding your community also means that you seek support in testing times. If you are going through any setbacks such as divorce, illness, parenting problems, grief, etc., besides seeking professional help, be sure to connect with those who can support you through your trials.

October 9, 2020, was unfortunately the day I become a sweet little Type 1 diabetic's mom. As I was in the hospital with my little girl for about five days, I sat on my prayer rug in the middle of the night desperate to find support. I had very little knowledge and so did my family or friends. I felt lost and lonely. I began searching online and found a few T1D support groups and shared how I was feeling. People began to pour their hearts out and shared supportive, uplifting messages while I was still going through my initial shock. I immediately felt seen and heard, as if I was part of an exclusive group where everyone understood me and was ready to help. No one needs to do it alone. Asking for support is humbling and necessary for our difficulties.

In fact, anything big or small, fun or challenging, can become easier and more relatable with like-minded others. Stay connected with the community that understands your struggle as you can get and offer support where needed. It can be quite lonely and frustrating if you try to get that level of understanding or reliance from anyone who has no connection to your experience.

Now, sometimes, there can be way too many groups, especially in online spaces. So, before you go joining random groups and feel lost in there somewhere, be sure to know your specific needs. When I was looking for groups to join for T1D, I found some groups with a lot of oversharing, complaining, depressing, negative energy. I decided I didn't need that at all. I wanted to embrace my journey and practice *radical acceptance* along with empowerment so I can lovingly take care of my girl with this special condition. And after much research, I found a couple of supportive groups and podcasts filled with positive energy and helpful content that were more aligned with my needs and mindset. So, I unfollowed what wasn't useful to me. Before you go looking for your people, here are the questions to ask yourself:

- *What* qualities am I looking for in a new connection, supporter, or mentor? Am I looking for a good listener? Am I seeking expert knowledge to move my career or hobby or other ambition to the next level? Or am I looking to offer my expertise to others? Do I want to collaborate and network with others?

- *Where* can I find my people? In the local community? Networking groups? What kinds of events can I attend? Which online groups can I explore? Which platform is best for what I need?

- *Who* can I ask for help? This can be the most important question after you know what you want. Who can I strike a conversation with about this?

Reflect

1. List the communities you are currently a part of.
2. Which ones do you need to exit?
3. Where do you need to find connection with others?
4. What actions can you take to find the right people that meet your needs?

It all begins and ends in your mind. What you give power to, has power over you.

—Leon Brown

Adopt a Growth Mindset

Your mindset is a set of beliefs that affect how you understand yourself and the world. It influences how you think, feel, and behave in any given situation. Our minds have immense power over our lives. Modern psychology knows about how belief systems regarding our own abilities and potential fuel our behaviours and determine our success in life. A lot of this understanding stems from the work of renowned psychologist Carol Dweck, detailed in her book *Mindset: The New Psychology of Success.* She explains how the power of our beliefs, both conscious and subconscious, can have profound impact on nearly every aspect of our lives. She also highlights how we can change our preprogramed thought process and adopt a mindset that serves us well in life.

> *When you enter a mindset, you enter a new world. In one world (the world of fixed traits) success is about proving you're smart or talented. Validating yourself. In the other (the world of changing qualities) it's about stretching yourself to learn something new. Developing yourself.*
>
> —Carol S. Dweck, *Mindset: The New Psychology of Success* (Dweck 2007)

Importance of Your Mindset

Your mindset dominates your life. Most life coaches primarily focus on shifting their client's mindset prior to beginning any practical work. It is your paradigm, your programing, your power. How you see any situation depends on your inner beliefs. One of the most basic beliefs we carry about ourselves has to do with how we view our personality. How we see the world depends hugely on how we see ourselves. What we do in life and the choices we make are dependent on our mindsets. How we process setbacks and how much effort we put in also depend on our mindsets. Our mindsets determine whether we are stuck in our ways or are open to exploring new ideas and opportunities.

Your mindset can either be supported by an internal monologue of persistent judgement based on previous evidence of what is possible, or by seeking, learning, and allowing constructive action which promotes continual growth. It is your mindset that holds you as hostage to your limiting paradigm, keeping you stuck in old ways. And it is your mindset that unlocks your ability to pursue new goals ambitiously. Anything you currently struggle with in life can be approached mindfully by evaluating your mindset. It sounds simple, yet an *inner shift* in your personal beliefs and psychology can drastically transform your life.

Fixed versus Growth Mindset

Do you wonder why some people easily take chances, feel more confident, try new challenging things, and pursue their dreams while others find it very hard? The later may blame their personality or ability for their difficulty. In actuality, their mindset is to be blamed. You predominately either have a fixed mindset or a growth mindset.

A *fixed mindset* assumes that our character, intelligence, and creative ability are given characteristics that we can't change in any meaningful way. Therefore, success is the affirmation of that inherent intelligence. This belief basically suggests that *success is for the lucky, skilled, smart few and not for everyone.* In many ways, our society instills such concepts into our subconscious minds. We are compared to our siblings and peers at home and in schools as well as in workspaces. Our strengths and potentials for growth are rarely highlighted. We develop low competency as we compare ourselves to others. Our self-beliefs impact our self-esteems negatively.

For individuals with a fixed mindset, mistakes indicate lack of ability. They may be discouraged easily, get threatened by others' success, take criticism personally, and consider themselves to be failures. Their self-beliefs such as, I won't ever improve, leads them to thinking, Why should I even bother? From that belief follows a self-destructive downward spiral which leads to unhappiness, lack of confidence, low self-esteem, and stagnation in life.

A *growth mindset*, on the other hand, sees opportunity for growth and potential for stretching one's existing abilities. It thrives on challenge and sees failure not as evidence of unintelligence but as a chance to learn and grow. The belief this mindset carries is, *if I don't give up, I can achieve my goal*. This mindset can be learned through an individual's encouraging upbringing or influence through one's life, and it can also be self-developed with conscious awareness and effort.

A growth mindset doesn't limit oneself to what might be possible, rather it looks for expanding that capacity. Individuals with a growth mindset develop talents, persist when facing setbacks, and look for problem solving instead of giving up, promoting continual growth and success. It may seem farfetched for some, yet very appealing and powerful. Well, here's the good news, anyone can adopt a growth mindset.

> *Few people realize that they are held prisoner by their own paradigm. Even fewer realize they hold the key that unlocks the cell door.*
>
> —Bernadette Logue, *Unleash your Life*

When children have a growth mindset, they tend to have a hunger for learning and a desire to work hard and discover new things. This often translates into academic achievement. This can be a natural inclination and can also be learned. Parents need to be careful though, as they can also promote a fixed mindset by telling the child what "should" be pursued. And I know this might come as a surprise to many, but according to Dweck, labelling your child as "smart" can sometimes promote a fixed mindset. It sends a message to the child that they either have an ability or they don't, and that there is nothing they can do to change that fact. If they believe to be smart, they experience pressure to prove it and if they don't feel smart, they will think that they aren't good enough, which might diminish their effort. (Dweck 2007)

A way to tactfully compliment your child is to praise their efforts, not results. By focusing on the process rather than the outcome, adults can help kids understand that their efforts and hard work can lead to achieving whatever they set out to attain.

Question Your Mindset

Our mindset is manifested from a very young age and determines a great deal of our behaviour, our relationship with success and failure (professionally as well as personally), and our capacity for happiness in life. When we are young, how we are directly or indirectly taught to think, shapes our mindsets. Any major life situation can alter our perception of our *self*. We must question the mindsets of our standardized society as well as our families, to understand how we developed ours.

The idealistic perception of growth in a society is often distorted. For example, in many traditional cultures, the idea of success is attaining a certain kind of job or accumulating heaps of wealth and high status. Imagine seeking that predetermined idea of success only to arrive at the end feeling unhappy and disconnected with yourself. Imagine gaining all wealth and meanwhile neglecting your health and family or ending up feeling lonely. So, we must question how we develop our mindsets in relation to our predisposed ideologies.

To pursue something you are internally unaligned with, can possibly be damaging. Acquiring a growth mindset doesn't mean we force ourselves to push our limits and strive to attain something that may not support our strengths or interests.

There is profound divine wisdom in the diverse intelligence humans are created with. Some intelligence is naturally gifted, and other can be learned or enhanced. Be sure to set your own goals and define what success means to you. Having the correct approach in your mind is not enough for success if you are chasing the wrong ambitions.

As a child, I felt incompetent in some ways when compared to siblings and peers. I was taught early on that *success* was a well-defined concept and a certain path to be followed. Becoming a doctor, engineer, or choosing a socially well-revered career was not enticing enough for me. I had hidden talents that I yearned to discover and enhance. But in an environment where my true strengths were not explored, I felt stuck. I didn't understand how growth could occur from a one-size-fits-all kind of fixed ideology. Because of this internal discord, I felt puzzled. Only to question it all as an adult!

Even though I struggled in the traditional educational system, my dad made sure I worked hard and made good grades. Despite the influence of many societal distortions, my dad exemplified a growth mindset in his life and hammered his version of this mindset into my subconscious mind, perhaps for me to then adopt it with my own understanding over time. He taught us to never stay stagnant and keep learning and growing in life. Our definitions of success may differ, but the mindset needed for growth on any path is the same. I came to my own understanding of how growth applies in my own journey.

Although in my upbringing I believed that there was competition and a race to becoming better than someone else, I now only focus on my personal goals, knowing very well that no one is comparable to my exact path. This mindset clears up a lot of distraction and allows for a more wholesome and enjoyable way of attaining personal goals. I know now that we all have unlimited potentials in our own unique ways and I'm busy challenging myself with an open mind.

Understanding how you developed your specific mindset, along all its limitations, is important for you to build your growth mindset. Question your mindset and challenge it. We all are a mix between fixed and growth mindsets in different ways. The more we shift towards adopting a growth mindset, the easier it becomes to overcome life's many challenges and see the possibilities this life and human potential offers.

Growth Mindset and Success

Everyone is not meant to pursue the same path to success. People possess different strengths that relatively allow them to pursue a myriad of things in life. Exploring your interests will allow you to discover your strengths. Think about your own definition of *success* and realize where you have potential for growth. If you passionately pursue your path, a growth mindset will be a huge advantage to you whereas a fixed mindset will debilitate you.

All you need is the self-belief that *you can* and anything you pursue thereafter with vigor and grit will bring you success in anything you seek to achieve. It is your distinctive journey of striving for your individualistic success that must be sought. Staying where you are should never be an option. A growth mindset requires evolving, learning, and seeking possibility in various aspects. You must learn to believe that you have the capacity for something better. You are never born with success; it is a continual process of development.

> *Becoming is better than being.*
> —Carol S. Dweck, *Mindset: The New Psychology of Success*

Our mindsets don't only translate into our success in personal and professional lives but also our relationships. A fixed mindset doesn't do well with conflicts within relationships and quickly assigns blame, whereas a growth mindset sees possibility for open communication and problem-solving as it seeks chances for development. This attitude gives opportunity for better understanding and deepening of relationships while earning trust and gaining humility.

A growth mindset also allows for challenging oneself to rectify one's shortcomings. A negative feedback received from an external source, can be seen as a powerful message to inspire you to self-reflect and look for self-improving solutions, as opposed to taking offense or avoiding such situations altogether. Every time you think with a growth mindset, you come back stronger and better with courage.

Working on challenging my client's attitudes allows me to help them build the right mindset needed to reflect on their pasts, overcome their limitations, help improve their relationships, and empower them to achieve their life goals. The more ownership we take of our paradigm, the more power we have.

Success can be easily attained with a growth mindset, no matter what you pursue in life. Are you wanting to lose weight and become a healthier version of yourself? You can do it! Are you wanting to attain a happier marriage? You can do it! Are you wanting to overcome your fear and expand your comfort zone? You can do it! Are you wanting to learn something new? You can do it! Are you wanting to pursue a new career? You can do it! Are you wanting to build your communication skills and grow your self-confidence? You can do it!

You must begin with believing that you are capable and leverage your mind's natural ability to learn, challenge, and grow. A growth mindset not only enhances your drive but also grows your self-esteem. And when facing adversities, one's positive mindset allows for problem-solving and overcoming challenges successfully. It allows for a person to see different perspectives and maintain an overall optimistic approach. It all begins with a positive imagination of oneself.

> *Our life is what our thoughts make of it . . . A man's true greatness lies in the consciousness of an honest purpose in life, founded on a just estimate of himself.*
> —Marcus Aurelius

If you research, you'll find that high-achieving individuals possess a growth mindset. They find their mistakes to be their biggest chances at getting better and smarter. Success starts with a state of mind. It comes down to your belief system, mainly about yourself and your capabilities. What you believe, you act on. You cannot act on something that you do not believe in. What you act on, you manifest. Any action you take results in some tangible consequence. What you manifest creates your reality. This is reliant on your personal paradigm, your mindset.

Ways to Attain a Growth Mindset

As a parent, I am very passionate about promoting a growth mindset in my children. Here are few things I teach my own and share with my clients:

- Use the word "yet." Instead of telling yourself you can't or you're not good at something say, Not yet, or, I'm working on this. Your choice of words impacts your actions, so inevitably, you will be motivated to improve any task to the best of *your* ability.

- Try to place more value on the process and not the end result. A growth mindset enjoys the learning process and subsequent progress. Any small improvements must be recognized and celebrated instead of being fixated on an expected time frame or outcome.

- Separate *improvement* from *failure*. Don't assume that "room for improvement" translates into failure. Replace the word *failure* with *learning.* Any time you make mistakes or fall short, think, What did I learn from this? And keep working on improvement instead of giving up.

- Analyze your mindset regarding a particular task or challenge. Assess your thought process and see how you can look at it in a way that is not self-limiting. Reframe any negativity into positivity. Ask for help if you need an external perspective.

- Try new things. Take risks and allow yourself to face your fears. Challenge yourself to go against your doubtful presuppositions. As you overcome your limitations, you'll obtain the right mindset and grow confidence.

Reflect

1. Assess your current mindset. In what ways is it fixed?
2. What kind of problems do you currently face due to your mindset?
3. What can you change to develop a growth mindset?

Live a life that is driven more strongly by curiosity than by fear.

—Elizabeth Gilbert

Face Your Fears

Notice, I didn't call this chapter "Overcome Your Fears." Even though the end goal is to overcome most of our self-generated, non-threatening fears; we do so by *facing* them first. Fearlessness is never a general goal. We are programed with the idea that somehow fear is shameful and cowardly and something to *overcome*. This whole idea itself is flawed as it goes against the way our minds have been designed.

We are meant to feel fearful of a threatening situation and have a fight-or-flight auto-response. It is how our brain protects us from real danger. However, the problem is that our brains don't really know what situations are essentially dangerous enough for us to become fearful of. That is what we want to recognize and train our minds to learn and accurately deal with.

Understanding Fear

In order to arrive at an elevated level of self-awareness, we need to understand how our minds work. How are thoughts generated? Why do we get anxious? What beliefs bring about our fears? And how do we face our fears with our new awareness?

There are different kinds of fears. I want to primarily discuss the concept of fear concerning self-growth. To become a better achiever in life, we must learn to deal with our self-sabotaging and compelling fears. But before that, we need to realize how these fears are generated and perceived by us. Many of our fears of the unknown are our impulsive negative thoughts which are based on evidence from our past judgements. Therefore, majority of our fears and anxieties are caused by inadequate management of our imagination and can just be false alarms.

If we are not in a real danger situation, where fear can be of great benefit to us, we need to identify it as something we can recognize and work with. Our brain knows how to react to fear; however, it doesn't recognize whether the fear should exist in that situation or not. So, it could deal with a real dangerous situation, such as climbing up a steep mountain the same way as anxiety before an interview. Climbing a dangerous mountain can be a fearful undertaking, whereas an interview is nothing to fear, rather to face, keeping all outcomes in mind. If we are unaware, our brain simply knows that it is dealing with fear and produces the same response every time something is unknown, challenging, or stressful. We must identify the reality of the fears we face in different situations and process them accordingly.

> *The fears we don't face become our limits.*
> —Robin Sharma

We become accustomed to believing in certain fears and react to them by creating limitations for ourselves. Many people fail before they give themselves a fair enough chance to succeed merely because of their fears. It immobilizes too many and prevents them from achieving what they desire and are capable of.

Being fearful of social situations, such as public speaking or performing in front of an audience, can be daunting for most people. However, if you really think about it, such a situation is not one to be feared as there really isn't a real threat to deal with. Still, we experience our heart racing, our stomach cramping, our throat feeling lumpy, and extreme nervousness. These responses are simply reactions due to some chemical changes that go on inside our brains when feeling threatened. But what makes us feel that way? It is simply the fear of failing or being judged. We need to understand that our anxieties are uncomfortable, but not dangerous.

Logically speaking, at the most, someone would judge us negatively, or reject us, or we might feel embarrassed or incompetent. It really can't get that bad! In such situations, our self-generated anxiety can rob us of opportunities and possibilities if we give up. This is where an act of courage is needed to be practiced. Unless there is something to be feared, there is no opportunity for courage. It is when we practice courage that we enhance our confidence through facing our fears. So, we must reframe such fears and look at them as opportunities to practice courage.

Courage is knowing what not to fear.
—Plato

Fear of Rejection

Like most people, I struggled with the *fear of rejection*. I wanted to please everyone and be liked and accepted by everyone. This expectation got me into a few unhappy situations and kept me small. My self-generated perception existed within myself, and I had to learn to unpack it and let it go. It took me a few years to grow out of that thinking habit and reprogram myself to become okay with the idea of not being understood or accepted or liked.

I came to realize that we are not always going to be in full alignment with another person. Therefore, some things will be rejected and not always be received how we intended to. Letting go of our desire to be accepted helps us ascend to the next level of attaining acceptance of ourselves as we live our truth. Our desire to be authentic must be greater than our need to be liked. Having the fear of being judged or misunderstood can hold us back from being our true self.

In overcoming our fear of rejection, we must also learn to not pursue certain things just because others will approve of them. Instead, chase our own goals and develop the courage to be in sync with who we are and want to become. When we are self-driven, we allow room for mistakes and overcome the fear of failure. And in situations where we do receive negative judgement or constructive feedback, such as in an interview, we learn to frame it in a way that helps us grow. It could provide necessary information for us to move forward. It could push us to analyze things in new light and shift our focus for the better. Fear of rejection is not dangerous and should never limit us.

Triggers of Fear

How does fear come about? When our mind considers anything a threat, it generates alarming feelings of fear and avoids it all together. Some potential triggers that enhance fear can be uncertainty, change, or struggle. These things are present in any real dangerous situations as well as in situations where learning and growth thrives. Anytime you want to be creative, try new things, be in a new situation, you naturally want to play it safe. Our mind likes to choose the easier route. We must train our minds to feel the fear and take on challenging situations with courage because that is when we expand ourselves. We must learn to negotiate with fear and see where it takes us.

I'm not saying be fearless and overcome the *feeling* of fear. I want us to take away the shame and worry around that feeling. When we think we are not supposed to feel fear, we avoid it altogether. That is when we avoid taking progressive action and hold ourselves back from taking any risks. Soon as we embrace that fear will be there, we accept the feeling with our new upgraded approach. We learn to transcend our fear by daring bravely and giving it a new definition: *Something not to get rid of but rather experience and build courage for.*

Psychologically, once you can develop competency around something, you can build more confidence around it. There was a time I hated speaking up in a classroom or in front of an audience. Now, I purposely put myself in situations where I can expand my comfort zone, make some mistakes, learn from them and keep moving on. I realized that without making my mistakes, I won't be able to grow. This works for anything in life when you make the decision to not limit yourself and instead challenge yourself regardless of feeling the fear of the unknown, which will always be there. In order to face our fears, we need to acknowledge them and understand why they exist.

Out of the many things I learned from author, high performance coach, and personal development leader Brendon Burchard, I learned that there are three main reasons that trigger fear (I'll share the expanded form of my notes from his YouTube videos in my own words):

The ***fear of loss:*** When we fear of losing something in the process of trying anything new or stepping into the unknown. In the attempt to try anything new, there is the possibility of losing something about the lifestyle, job, security, predictability, friends, comfort, etc. The fear of losing anything causes people to not act towards something that might be good for them. Many people don't change because of that fear of loss. They want to stay comfortable and repeat what's already known and *easy* as opposed to feeing challenged towards something *better*. If you focus on what you are gaining instead of what you lose, you'll experience change positively. Challenging yes, but that is how we develop ourselves.

The ***fear of process***: When we are fearful of all the handwork we must do to achieve something. If you want to start a business, write a book, lose some weight, become educated, learn a craft, or anything else, work is always needed. This fear is basically due to the bad habit of laziness and wanting to stay comfortable. We must overcome that mindset of avoiding work and having to discipline ourselves. The possibilities of growth are endless when we can instill self-discipline and expand our comfort zones. We are competent beyond measure; but if we let our feelings of "This is new and scary and hard" overpower us, then we can become very weak, lazy, and limited. Sure, quitting a bad habit, having to exercise, changing diet, or adopting new schedules, etc. can be difficult. But that is how we achieve better things and gain confidence.

The ***fear of outcome***: This one is a very prevalent frame of thought—the fear of failure! What if the grass is not greener? What if my investment is wasted? What if it's not better on the other side on the fence? All the *what ifs* trick our minds into losing. This one affects most people due to their poor imagination of what *could* happen as well as their poor expectation of what *should* happen. I have struggled with this one personally and over time, I shifted my mindset and started to take new challenges as I began to think win-win. Whether you succeed in the end or learn from mistakes, you're still a winner. That is a solid mind-shift we all must adopt in order to face our fears. Gaining any kind of experience through the *process* of change is valuable to anyone. With that belief, you can overcome your self-doubts and face any fears that emerge.

Mind-Shifting and Reframing

In any new situation in life, there is always an element of risk involved. But if your fears overwhelm you, then you allow them to overpower you. We need to identify which fears are causing serious limitations in our lives. From being more vulnerable in social situations to taking new lifestyle challenges, we must evaluate the true dangers and deal with our fears head on using our optimistic imagination.

> *What if I fall? Oh, but my darling, what if you fly?*
> —Erin Hanson

Think about possible positive outcomes of the change instead of magnifying the fears in your mind. Imagine all the excitement around that new lifestyle, the new feeling, the achievement, where it can take you etc. Keep the end goal in mind. Focus on possibility and you will overcome the unnecessary fears. For anything you anticipate in future, visualize a positive outcome. It really is a mind game here. Because even if you end up disappointed in the end, you will happily take the lessons and keep moving forward.

Elizabeth Gilbert in her book *Big Magic* talks about this with a beautiful letter to fear. I love how she says that we need to keep fear in the back seat of our car as it is forbidden to drive us even though it accompanies us always. She adds, "As we ride together with creativity and fear, we advance into the terrifying yet marvelous terrain of unknown outcome." (Gilbert 2016)

We can't get rid of fear, but we don't allow it to lead us in life. We can use it as a tool to help us make decisions and take necessary actions towards our goals. It is certainly not there to keep us inactive and hold back from trying the unknown.

A habit we need to tackle when it comes to dealing with our fears is *overthinking.* The more we feed the idea of possible fears, the more vivid an illusion we generate and believe to be true. Most of the things we fear never materialize. It is our fears that create doubts and self-limiting beliefs in our minds. As we get a good grasp on our fears, we build self-reliance and are less intimidated to pursue our dreams, live our truth, and accomplish difficult things.

Your fears see every challenge as a threat. When you reframe these threats as opportunities to experience and learn through, you can do anything. Feel the fear and try the next new thing that will grow your courage and build your confidence.

How to Face Your Fears

Here are some strategies to try in attempts to face your fears:

- Bring awareness towards the fear and gain a sense of reality of your fear. Is it really as bad as you feel? What could be the worst outcome? The more you prepare yourself to deal with your fear, the smaller it becomes.

- Visualize a positive outcome for whatever you attempt to accomplish. Imagine what success looks and feels like more and more to overcome your fears.

- Check for evidence. Do you have real evidence for your fears or are you making scary guesses? Has such a fear been overcome by others? Explore how. Allow that to be your evidence to face your fears.

- Educate yourself. We are most fearful of the unknown. If your fear is based on a lack of information, then get the knowledge you need to examine the situation based on facts rather than mere speculation.

- Follow someone who has done it before and knows the answers you are looking for. Find them, ask them, learn from them and watch your fears slowly shrink.

- Stay positive. Check your attitude. Are you expecting the worst? Your attitude makes all the difference so be sure to keep that in check.

Reflect

1. What are your fears that are limiting you in life? Make a list.

2. How will you reframe your biggest fear positively in order to face it?

3. How would it feel to overcome your fear?

4. Where can you seek help and support?

We first make our habits, and then our habits make us.

—John Dryden

Improve Your Habits

I didn't quite understand the big hullabaloo behind a mid-life crisis when I heard of the idea in my twenties. But as you age beyond early thirties, you begin to understand the importance of time, youth, good health, habits, purpose, everything . . . well, if you become aware! The sooner one begins to value these things, the better. How we lead our lives matters. Our morning and evening routines matter. Our habitual consumption of food, media, and influence of other people, all matter. Our thinking and feeling habits matter.

We all acquire good and bad habits, which determine our quality of life. At their worst, habits can run you in the wrong direction without you even realizing what's happening. And when you're set in your ways, the damage is hard to undo without putting in a lot of work to build better habits.

Good habits, however, take you in a positive direction and you control the ride. You reap what you sow! If you are a healthy eater, you probably have very healthy food-choice habits. If you're fit, you likely have good exercising habits. If your house is tidy and organized, then you have developed good disciplinary habits. In fact, all successful people seem to share the common trait of good habits in many aspects of their lives. Successful people aren't any smarter or better than anyone else, but their habits drive them towards more knowledge, competence, and skills; therefore, more control over their lives and enjoyable results.

The Compound Effect

Everything we do adds up and has a compound effect on our lives. This is a very important concept explained well in Darren Hardy's book, *The Compound Effect*. Hardy talks about the impact of *"the progressive accumulation" of small actions taken consistently over time,* leading you to success or adversity. These actions are based on your everyday choices. "The real cost of a four-dollar-a-day coffee habit over 20 years is $51,833.79. That's the power of the Compound Effect." (Hardy 2012)

Now, compounding good habits takes a lot of patience. And that's a problem because in today's times, humans aren't trained for patience. We're programmed for instant gratification. The social pressures to keep up with others, even when we knowingly make poor long-term decisions, are very real and hard to overcome. But we must make our *inner shift* by taking responsibility for our choices.

Observe your day-to-day habits and how they affect you over time. Your daily choices make you the person you are. Just think about it, a thirty-minute walk daily can improve your mood and promote physical activity, cutting out sugar and choosing a low-carb diet can feel healthier and leads to dramatic weight loss, a couple minutes regular morning meditation can help overcome anxiety and calm your mind, saving a small amount of money regularly can add up to a large sum over time. You want your small, good habits to become an automatic system for you that eventually generates positive results.

When one builds the discipline to make changes in one area of life, they can begin to see the impact at large. Hardy refers to this phenomenon as "the ripple effect". You make one right choice, and you'll see results multiplied based on that choice. You choose poorly, you'll have to work harder to undo the damage and change your choices. If you don't mindfully choose what's right for your life goals, then you unintentionally make the choice to passively receive whatever comes your way.

Darren Hardy mentioned that the compound effect is the combination of multiple attributes that are needed to develop better habits. His formula is:

Compound Effect = Choices + Behavior + Habits + Time

The strategy for gaining massive rewards from small changes requires persistence, responsibility, and accountability. To make the compound effect work, we need to make the right choices, develop a responsible behavior, cultivate the best habits, and stay consistent over time.

> *The best deeds are those done consistently.*
> —Prophet Muhammad (peace be on him)

Healthy Holistic Habits

Habits are our automatic behaviours that we acquire overtime. They put us on autopilot mode in many aspects of our daily lives. Think about how little thought you put into brushing your teeth, showering, or driving. Because habits require little conscious energy, they can free us to focus our mental energy on more creative endeavours. But to start a new habit, one must consciously work on it and practice it repeatedly until it becomes an unconscious behaviour.

When I talk to my clients, I take a holistic approach to life coaching. I always ask them questions about their lifestyles, as I know the ripple effects of their day-to-day habits are at play. Our daily choices and habits have a huge impact upon both our levels of happiness and success. Establishing healthy habits, like eating a nutrient rich diet, getting plenty of sleep, and participating in regular exercise, can dramatically change how you feel. Our habits impact our relationships, how we view our lives, and how much effort we are willing to put into any self-work.

Good holistic habits are needed to help manage our overall lifestyle. It can be very easy to live the "normal western lifestyle" which consists of mostly staying indoors, harmful postures, prolonged hours on a screen, lack of exercise, and foods with minimal nutritional value. What's readily available to you is not the best for your general well-being. You must make the conscious effort to build your healthy habits and choose a more holistic lifestyle, which includes, your mind, body, and soul.

Be a life-long student. Enrich your mind with great literature. Learn new things and connect with people of experience and knowledge. Be cognizant what you feed your mind. Challenge yourself to acquire a new skill, read something different, or search about something new. Learning keeps our minds engaged and sharp, even into old age. Pay attention to your habitual thought patterns and reflect on them regularly.

Move, move, and move more! Add a few regular pockets of movement into your day. Get out and indulge in the healing powers of the morning sunshine. Watch the sky and enjoy the sunsets. Walk, hike, run. Join the gym and stay consistent. Movement alone adds many high impact benefits to our mundane lifestyles. Develop a regular easy-to-follow routine to stay active.

Cut out unhealthy eating habits. The prepackaged, processed, high carbs, genetically modified, too sugary or too salty, fried or preserved foods need to be eliminated. Try to consume real home-cooked meals and be conscious of the nutritional value of your diet. Add a green smoothie and healthier snacks such as nuts and fruits to fuel you through the day and to avoid unhealthy cravings.

Introduce a few soul-enriching practices into your day. Try building a habit of offering regular prayers and a brief meditation practice with uninterrupted quiet time. Develop a few rituals that create peace and calm through your day such as watching the sunrises and sunsets, deep breathing, creating art, gardening or writing down your thoughts or feelings. Consider developing an easy-to-follow morning and evening routine which bring you joy.

Know that it's never too late to introduce new habits into your life. The more you are open to change, the more opportunity you'll find and the more you will grow in different ways.

Habits Create Success

When asked, many people say that their number one goal in life is to be happy. Success and happiness are related, however, what matters is how we define "success" for ourselves. It isn't something only measured by one's bank balance or worldly accomplishments, because many people achieve those goals and still don't feel happy. One needs to aim for a holistic approach to success, which in turn provides one with true fulfilment.

Most people don't know this, but you feel as successful as the quality of your life and relationships. Building healthy habits leads to improving the quality of your daily life, which will help develop self-confidence and overall contentment. As a result, this also refines your relationships. The truth is that, you can only give from what you have. If you feel unhealthy, unworthy, and unhappy, you can't have thriving relationships. When you develop great personal habits, you also inspire others around you.

It can be challenging to move out of old, unhealthy habits and build good habits. Many times, we have a *self-limiting belief* issue, where we think we can't change. The truth is, you can shift any belief about your potential at any time by starting to create small new habits and slowly making them permanent. Limitations, after all, only exist in your mind.

> *There are no constraints on the human mind, no walls around the human spirit, no barriers to our progress except those we ourselves erect.*
>
> —Ronald Reagan

Once you begin to choose a better version of yourself, you must take action to prove yourself right. Here's a rule I learned: *choose better over easy*. For example, eating out is easy; cooking healthy meal is better. We're always presented with this choice. The problem is, easy is fast, fun, and comfortable and we are wired to lean in that direction. But we gain rewards by choosing *better*, not necessarily by choosing hard. *Better* can be a wholesome choice if we go for it with the correct attitude.

Here's a tip: reframe by asking yourself, What is good for me? You can also try asking, What am I worth? and give it some deep thought before acting upon your pre-programed inclinations. Chances are that you'll always come to the conclusion that you deserve better. When you choose a better version of yourself mindfully, you develop healthier habits and attain success.

How to Become Productive

Many people struggle with procrastination and lack productivity. These are also habitual behaviours that can be consciously shifted. Habits are not built aimlessly. Think about scheduling your day before your head hits the pillow or early in the morning. This is one of my most common tips. From experience, I can tell you that one of the most common reasons for failure is that people either don't schedule at all or schedule too much into their day. It can get overwhelming for many. You can schedule time slots for specific tasks and stick to them, so you feel productive as you habitually accomplish small tasks.

Making a quick list of a few things you want to accomplish in your day will help you sleep better and wake up with ideas and flow of positive energy to fulfill your goals. Also, I recommend scheduling just a couple hours of uninterrupted productive work each day on your big goals or major project of choice. Try to stay focused and avoid distractions during this time. Sit at a place where you can feel most productive. Staying consistent is hard work and requires constant effort, but very well worth it. To get more ideas to build and maintain healthy habits, *read books like Atomic Habits and The Power of Habit.*

> *Good habits are hard to form but easy to live with. Bad habits are easy to form and hard to live with.*
> —Brian Tracy

Keep It Simple

People are often scared to build new habits because they assume it will be hard and they won't be able to continue and fail. Start very small and try to sustain good habits. Some examples of my simple good habits are drinking warm water in the morning, caring for my plants, daily stretches/yoga, praying as a family, daily expressing gratitude, sharing at least one positive reminder on my social media, supplications before bed, listening to beneficial podcasts during my drives/workouts, etc. These are just little things, but they add up and become your lifestyle.

The idea of small changes compounding over time can be contrasted with attempting to make big sudden changes. A common example is when people aim to lose weight and start exercising. They often declare a big goal and start with extreme changes like dieting or going to the gym daily. But this is often unsustainable. Once you miss a few times, you get discouraged and end the whole effort. Instead, small changes build consistency and momentum as they form new habits that you can slowly maintain long-term, which will help propel you to success.

Consider beginning by simply bringing awareness towards your daily habits. Make a list of things you want to work on. Are you spending countless hours sitting around wasting time watching TV or scrolling on your phone? Do you sit on a desk for long hours? Do you get fresh air and sun every day? How about your sleep quality? Do you have any standards set for food choices? Do you exercise? What are your facial expressions, body language, posture, and word choices like? What are your repetitive thoughts? Write down anything that comes to mind in order of importance. Bring your focus towards the most needed changes in your current habits.

Work on your mindset a little bit. Once you have the awareness that a change is required for your overall well-being and happiness, you can start small. Here's the thing, we think we either *have* good habits or we don't, which is why people have the common excuse, "But I've always been this way . . ." We must realize that at some point in time, we have created and established our bad habits. Our brain either works for us or against us. Our job is to understand how we can get it to work *for* us. One way is to develop the belief that *what I admire is possible for me and I am willing and responsible to play my part*. Here are some easy tips:

- Challenge yourself to build one new habit for a month.
- Combine a difficult habit with something enjoyable to you. For example, listen to your favourite podcast while working out.
- Notice the distractions and demotivators and eliminate them. If your phone distracts you when you try to build a reading habit, keep the phone outside of the room.

- Make a plan that works for you to achieve this goal and commit to it.
- Start by taking small consistent steps and build on.
- Track your progress and hold yourself accountable.
- Get others involved so it becomes harder to back down.

> *95% of everything you do is the result of habit.*
> —Aristotle

Reflect

1. Think of a current goal in your life. What is a bad habit that is holding you back from attaining this goal?
2. How can you change this bad habit by creating a healthier one in its place?
3. Think about what additional related habits you can add on.

The ego is only an illusion, but a very influential one. Letting the ego-illusion become your identity can prevent you from knowing your true self.

—Wayne Dyer

Befriend Your Ego

Ego is one of my favourite things to examine. The more we understand our ego, the more masterful we become with ourselves. The question is, what is *ego?* And the answer is not simple. I can share my knowledge of the ego based on some of my own ego-vigilant reflective self-work and research. I am fascinated with the power of ego, and I think it can be such a vague concept, however, with deep inner awareness one can really get a good grasp on the infamous thing.

What Is Ego?

To sum it up in an easy definition is difficult. Some people would say that the ego doesn't exist as they have never seen it. Others might think that everything about them is simply a part of their personality. Most people think *having an ego* is a negative trait. The ego may be blamed for many problems and is often labelled as the *enemy*. We have heard of books written on this aspect such *Ego is The Enemy* by Ryan Holiday, which discuss the self-centered concept we normally attribute to ego. The antidote to which is attaining humility and thinking beyond oneself. Such understanding suggests that you either *have* an ego or not.

The truth is, we all have an ego-self. To begin to understand the concept of our ego, we need a self-reflective process to look inward in a way that we see parts of our behaviours, emotions, and thoughts in a different light than mere personality traits. Each one of us also possesses a dark side which can be explored through diving into the unconscious aspects of ourselves that are responsible for our impulsive reactions and projections. Doing some intentional *shadow work* can be helpful to really understand how our ego plays out.

When trying to understand our ego, we need to drop the excuses such as, That is just the way I am, or, I'm like this because of my parents or childhood. These excuses make parts of our personality appear fixed and unchangeable. In fact, this may be hard to understand, but those voices in our heads are part of the ego as well. They narrate a story of an unchangeable and helpless self. When our goal is attaining self-mastery, there is very little room for blaming and unconscious reliance on pre-programed thoughts, which primarily feed our egos. We must question and challenge such thoughts.

Ego seems to be an abstract, hard-to-define concept, especially because it is commonly used to define a very particular aspect of human personality. The other complication is that the ego has many means of expression. It shows up in unfamiliar ways and impacts our minds and emotions accordingly. Most of us are unconsciously allowing the ego to take the lead in our lives.

Growing up, we are shaped by our environment, which asks us to be a certain way. Our society feeds us a very egocentric way of conducting ourselves. We believe in man-made timelines, standards, competitions, comparisons, and predetermined notions for success in life, which plague our minds and hearts. But *conscious living* is a whole different ball game! It requires awareness and a deeper connection with our minds and souls. It opens the possibility of choosing how we want to conduct ourselves in a way that is free of our preceding paradigm. We must make the choice to unlearn things and discover the rebirth of a soulful, higher self.

Most of us are raised to believe that our labels are important. We don't really understand *why* at a younger age, so we develop a thought pattern unconsciously that drives us while keeping us empty on the inside. Are you intelligent or stupid? Are you successful or a failure? Our internal dialogue of thoughts become opinions, causing self-rejection and criticism. Much of our time, energy, and efforts in this world seem to be directed at chasing the positive labels of intelligence and success. We are also running away from the negative labels: "stupid," "loser," and "failure." Such labels have deep rooted beliefs and emotional value attached to them, which is what makes us show up the way we do.

The game of *labels* and *image* is set up by the *ego*. It keeps us trapped in expectations of our identity and cycles of emotions. You always seem to be running after the next big thing to prove your success and maintain your labels. Or you run away from things to dodge other negative labels. There is always something to prove to others or some way to compare with others.

On one extreme, you want to look a certain way, physically or intelligently, to maintain your *image*. You want to be right and win the arguments to prove you have knowledge and correct opinions. You can't accept mistakes. You seek praise and want to be known for your successes. You fall into perfectionism. You don't feel you need to learn anything from someone else, be criticized, or be corrected. You are obsessed with winning, even in board games! Your ego may lead you to prove yourself.

And then there's the other end of the ego spectrum, where you need to always rely on other's approvals. A new perspective triggers you. An unknown concept makes you uncomfortable. You choose to stay comfortable with what you know and avoid challenges. You are the way you are and that's what you tell yourself. You fear confrontations and voicing your opinions. Bending the rules terrifies you. You want to stay safe. You follow crowds and don't want to stick out. Your ego may lead you to stay small and not apply yourself fully. These are all possible manifestations of your ego. All humans possess a variety of ego driven behaviours that are specific to their own psychology.

So, basically, the ego is working to control your attention by its judgement on how you compare to others in different ways. It creates a war within yourself as it constantly competes with others and/or the standards of society. Let me list some general manifestations and resulting dangers of ego:

- It needs to be known, seen, and heard.
- It can make us feel small, needy, or not good enough.
- It keeps us comparing with others and promotes arrogance or discontentment.

- It prevents us from learning or seeking advice or help.

- It makes us take offence to any criticism or "ugly truths" about ourselves.

- It makes us fear loss and attaches us to our image or worldly possessions.

- It causes superiority or inferiority complexes within us.

- It keeps us from having clarity and being authentic.

- It robs us of having humility and gratitude.

- It makes us live on autopilot mode and not question things.

The above seems *a lot* but still doesn't reveal all the facets and layers of the ego. We are merely scratching the surface here. If you can relate to any of the above, don't worry—most humans do, as we all have egos and it's normal. Confronting the ego, and not letting it control our lives, is a rare undertaking. A good chunk of my coaching sessions comprises of understanding and managing the ego-driven tendencies and how they play out in our lives, which makes this my favourite topic to discuss on a deeper level.

Unpacking Our Ego

Your ego creates a self-image where you find yourself better or less than others. Your ego yearns for *self-importance*. Everyone develops an ego growing up early in life. Any praise, criticism, or trauma—of any amount—can play a part in developing your ego. Anything true or false about your self-understanding, as a younger person, adds to your ego—a lot of which is simply a projection of someone else's ego, mostly your parents. You can estimate then how inaccurate and distorted your egoistic self-beliefs can be. And to live a life enslaved to the ego-based tendencies is such tragedy!

Understanding your ego as you grow into an adult and continue to add to your ego-self is mandatory for deep self-awareness and constant growth. This process includes, knowing how healthy your ego is, how it can be destructive and cause misery in your life, and how you can use this information about your ego to heal yourself and transform your life exceptionally. I call this process *befriending your ego!*

We mostly hear of the ego in self-praising, arrogant contexts. However, the times when we are too shy or fearful of expressing our truths, we are serving our ego. This is when we begin to feel like we are not good enough or are less than in comparison to others in some way. Self-acceptance, as well as self-rejection, are automatic parts of your belief system and your ego identity. Your fear of being seen and known, or being raw and real, is truly because of submitting to the ego.

What makes you arrogant at times? And at other times, what makes you feel insecure and weak? What serves the infamous thought, *What will people think?* which makes you overthink and worry about how people perceive you. What makes you obsessively self-judgemental or overly critical of yourself? What is it that doesn't allow you to surrender and let go of things? What keeps you from growing and changing, as it narrates a story of "This is who I am because x y z" in your mind, as a result, keeping you stuck? Your job is to find that story deep within as you shift inwards and gain ego-awareness.

People always judge others based on ego. This happens mostly with conversations and arguments. If someone disagrees with something you say, and they are motivated by the belief that they need to be seen more than you, implying that you should agree with them because *they are right.* This is an ego-based response. It doesn't allow one to agree to disagree. If they really think it through, and allow their mind to be open to receiving, they might find more *connection* as opposed to *correction,* and listen with curiosity. And if they disagree, they do so respectfully while sharing their authentic reasons. In most cases in life, there really can be more than one right answer, but when the ego is activated, we only see our own perspectives.

> *All you need to know and observe in yourself is this: Whenever you feel superior or inferior to anyone, that's the ego in you.*
> —Eckhart Tolle

Ego Awareness

Your ego is obsessed with labels and appearances. It could make you seek them or fear them. When it keeps you seeking, then chasing after your tainted perception of success, attaining acceptable status, and feeling superior may become your reality. When it holds you back, then self-loathing, lack of motivation, and feeling inferior become your reality. In either case, you never stop long enough to feel fulfilled, satisfied, or grateful in your life. The times when you allow the ego to control you, it is difficult to be content.

Don't get me wrong! Seeking success in life is something necessary and should be sought. However, our intention changes everything completely. What drives us is important. Is it our ego or our soul? That is the million-dollar question!

I have spoken about my people pleasing, low self-esteem days earlier. And a closer look only reveals to me that something I picked up innocently as a child navigating the world around me became a matter of *ego* as I grew older. As I broke through the shackles of ego-based narratives that played out in my life, I also became aware of where I picked some of my egoistic patterns from. Why was success defined in those ways? Why did I have to try so hard to be accepted? Why was it so difficult to be my authentic self? My inner child asks me these questions. I have allowed her to break through, heal, and reclaim her authenticity and lead soulfully.

Of course, my ego can be my enemy in many ways, but I am open to *befriending my ego*. What do I mean by that? If I have to live with its constant whisperings and hidden agendas, I would rather give it a friendly fight. I'm learning what drives it and what diminishes it. It is a part of me but not in control of me. If I see the ego as an enemy, I get to blame it and play victim to it. My only choice is to understand how it shows up for me and master ways to silence it and look beyond it.

This inner ego work takes deep awareness. Our egos manifest through our triggers, behaviours, attitudes, and mindsets. If we don't question them and lean in to understand what hints they present to us, we are enslaved to our ego and how it plays out. And when we lean in and recognize what secrets it possesses, we begin to befriend our ego while cautiously working against it and refining ourselves in the process.

If you want to read on the topic of ego, I recommend Eckhart Tolle's works, such as *Transcending the Ego*.

Ego Manifestation in Parenting

A lot of my coaching with parents revolves around ego work. It is our *ego* that gets in the way of soulful parenting. The biggest paradox in parenting is the ego! This insight will help you understand your relationship with your parents as well as your children. It can also enable some much-needed personal healing work. Perhaps it will then become easier for you to break any unhealthy patterns you may be repeating unconsciously in your current relationship with your children as well.

Conscious parenting requires ego awareness. Whereas unconscious parenting means to be unaware that we carry unique emotional stories and deeply rooted agendas that may be projected in our parenting styles. The parental ego is manifested by seeing our children as an extension of ourselves as opposed to independent individuals. With a conscious awareness of this tendency, parents will need to detach themselves from who their child is as a whole and understand their unique person, with distinctive needs and motivations.

When we become parents, we assume to know what is best for our child. Instead of knowing all the answers, understand that both parents and children continue to learn, heal, and grow throughout their lifetime. Parents feel responsible for providing guidance and being in control of their child. However, this *control* can quickly become corrupted if lead by their ego and dictated through projecting their own hurt, beliefs, unmet desires or expectations onto the child. This can show up as various intrusive or dismissive parenting patterns.

For many who grew up in households with lack of parental affection, emotional disconnect, or invalidation; parenting then unconsciously becomes an egoistic journey. It becomes an agenda we carry forth, which is less about listening and connecting to our children, and more about getting our personal needs met.

When we push our children to fulfill our own dreams and disallow them from pursuing their own passions and dreams, it is our ego at work. When we compare our children with our own upbringing, ego parenting is at play. When we expect them to act, learn and achieve based on standards we lay out, that's ego parenting. When we dismiss their needs that may be different from our own or their siblings, we lead with our egos.

If you want to break the cycle of ego-based generational behaviours, you must pause and reflect. Any reaction from you or your child is communicating an important message. Notice where your reactions are triggered by your own fears, wounds, or expectations from yourself or your child. And bring awareness towards how your egoistic behaviours impact your child. As you allow yourself to heal and intentionally break the unhealthy patterns, you will become more and more conscious and *connected* as a parent.

Attaining Soulfulness

Distinguishing where our egos can help us might take a lifetime mastering, but why not bring conscious awareness to this part of ourselves rather than blaming it? After all, your ego is there to guard you based on what it knows. But what it knows, needs to be questioned. Accepting a difficult part of you and challenging it allows you to become authentic. Therefore, when you act based on it, your ego can present itself as an enemy. Whereas, when you act against your ego, with awareness and grace, you can *befriend* it!

> *The strong are not those who defeat people. Rather, the strong are those who defeat their ego.*
> —Prophet Muhammad (Peace be upon him)

If we learn to befriend our ego, we can develop soulfulness, which is a journey to one's true *self*. In my personal journey, I realized that as I fall into the traps of the ego, I find myself taking offence, overthinking, and resisting change. The more I look beyond the ego-self and decide to be curious and soulful, the more I'm open to advice and rectification.

As I identify my egoistic inclinations, I'm able to make a conscious effort to go against the ego and cultivate humility. My gifts, successes, and experiences bring more gratitude instead of arrogance. The goal is to live in constant awareness of the ego-mind and challenge ourselves to negate its automatic responses in our behaviours.

When my ego begins to sabotage me with self-doubt, stress, aggressiveness, self-righteousness, shame, hypocrisy, jealousy, suspicion, or greed, I must observe it and remind myself that it is not the *essence* of me. In that moment, I need to create my *inner shift* from an ego-based being to a soul-based one with the awareness that my ego has become my enemy and might take over my thoughts, emotions, and actions. Awareness in and of itself is often the solution to any problem. You become aware that your ego has overpowered you and soon as you become aware, you take your power back!

How do you become aware? I truly believe that within each one of us, there exists a higher self, which is available for us to tap into. When we lead soulfully, without letting our thoughts or emotions guide us, we look at ourselves more neutrally and non-judgementally. We zoom out a little and open ourselves to see a bird's-eye view. And little things that may bother us, begin to really look very little in bigger scheme of things. We learn to take ourselves outside of the equation and look at things more holistically as opposed to being fixated on our small nuances. Your soulful self keeps a check on the ego with deeper awareness.

Practice shifting your awareness from the mundane, autopilot, external self to the sublime, conscious, inner self on a regular basis. Your ego presents some inner thoughts of the mind, which you can counter with your inner knowing of the soul. The ego can be a good friend, as it helps you train your consciousness. As a mere creation of the mind, society, and life events, the ego is not who you truly are and neither does it know your true self and its potential. So, your capacity to control the ego-based tendencies is far greater than the ego itself. Once you recognize that, you will be able to befriend your ego ever so consciously.

How to Transcend Your Ego

Any work related to your ego is a big undertaking. It is deep courageous work. Give yourself the credit for doing the self-work very few people are willing to do. Consider these things:

- Practice self-enquiry. Embrace your egoistic inclinations with curiosity and question their validity.
- Allow yourself to unlearn and relearn things about yourself, gradually shifting your ego-based manifestations.
- Refresh your perspective. Transition from an egocentric perspective to a soul-centered one. Revisit emotions of shame, stubbornness, gratification, anger, judgement, blame, etc. and silence them through deep inner awareness.
- Explore your potential to recognize, heal, and overcome your ego-based motivations.
- Once you understand how ego manifests in your life, take back the control. Your ego does its job by presenting some inner truths to you, and your job is to take charge from there.

Imagine the possibilities going forward when you develop a healthy ego-based perceptive about your true worth, confidence, and faith in your possibilities, free of comparisons with others. Embracing your personal magic and power.

Reflect

1. In what evident ways does your ego have a hold on you? Practice some ego-watching.

2. Reflect on your ego-based tendencies and how they are triggered.

3. Brainstorm ways you can challenge your ego and recover/break the pattern.

The best way to take care of the future is to take care of the present moment.

—Thick Nhat Hanh

Be Mindful

Our minds are powerful beyond measure. And the more powerful something is, the more dangerous it can be if we don't know how to work with it. If we let the mind work on autopilot mode for us, we will surely lose control and become enslaved to its habitual patterns, which are generated over time. Our minds are always working towards keeping us safe through falling back on how we train it to think unconsciously. The mind then works based on what it thinks we want by repeating our thinking patterns and therefore has tremendous capacity to overpower us. We can break free from the thought-habits of our minds by challenging it and creating new patterns intentionally.

One such pattern we all are accustomed to is ruminating the past or overthinking the future. These are our insecurities or anxieties lead by our ego. To the ego, present moment hardly exists. It feeds the two damaging thoughts to our minds that, What happened in the past has put limitations on me or was unfair and made me a victim, or, When this or that happens, I will finally be happy and peaceful. This projection of our past or future becomes a toxic pattern which prevents us from living the present. This pattern can be changed through becoming more mindful of our *now*.

The only moment that one can truly be sure of is the moment right now. If one spends that moment engrossed in the regrets from the past or worries for the future, then the present moment is wasted. You are dead in a wasted moment, as it doesn't even create a real memory, only refreshes the past or imagines the future, which just exist in the mind. You only truly live when you are aware that your reality is based on what's happening now.

In order to live more conscious and self-aware lives, we must begin to challenge our minds to fully live in the *current moment*. Many are fascinated and intrigued by the idea or practice of *mindfulness*, however, very few actually live that way. This *inner shift* alone can be transformational for anyone seeking a blissful life. One can learn a lot on this subject through the teachings of Eckhart Tolle. His book, *The Power of Now*, is great for a modern understanding on the subject of mindfulness, consciousness, and human ego.

> *In today's rush, we all think too much, seek too much, want too much, and forget about the joy of just being.*
> —Eckhart Tolle

What Is Mindfulness?

Mindfulness is the key pre-requisite that allows self-conscious inner work. It is an ancient practice which aligns with most religious teachings and is particularly relevant for modern life. It is a simplistic concept which, according to Jon Kabat-Zinn, requires us to pay attention in a conscious way: *on purpose, in the present moment, and non-judgementally*. It is practicing inward silence, which increases awareness, clarity, and acceptance of the reality of our present moment.

In Islamic practice, mindfulness refers to being God-conscious in remembering Him throughout the day with one's heart and mind, even while managing worldly affairs, aiming to show humility and seek His pleasure and rewards. It is attaining the state of awareness of oneself in relation to one's Master. In its purest form, it is the highest spiritual state that a believer can achieve. It essentially involves being present believers by habitually redirecting their attention to Allah Almighty through prayer and meditation extended to the entire lifestyle of the believer through the habits, routines, and supplications taught by Prophet Muhammad (peace be on him). Living mindfully for a Muslim then means to go through life deliberately as opposed to whim, unlike those with wandering minds who aimlessly go through life.

Unfortunately, most people in today's world are either living in the past or future, or occupying themselves with materialism, social media, Netflix, various compulsions, complexes, or comparisons. There are too many distractions for the human mind. We are stuck in cycles of *doing*. There's a meme online that says, "Because we have our *minds full,* we are less *mindful.*" We can't expect much joy, self-awareness, appreciation, peace, or compassion from a preoccupied and absent state of mind.

Mindfulness practices in your daily routine cut down the production of the stress hormones, reducing feelings of anxiety and promoting happiness. Being mindful helps us to train our attention. Our minds wander about most of the time, but every time we practice being mindful, we exercise our brains to become mentally fitter. We can take more control over our focus of attention rather than passively allowing our thoughts to take us away from the present moment.

An Intimidating Concept?

When I introduce this concept to my clients, they seem nervous as they expect it might require some skill and deep practice of stillness. They imagine a long, peaceful, uninterrupted meditation session and are really intimidated by the idea. In today's highly distracted environment, it can be very difficult to shift our minds inwards. I also had similar feelings years ago about practicing meditation. My head is always buzzing with thoughts and distractions. To empty my mind and focus on a given thing seemed like an enormous challenge. Also, I thought I'd get so bored and, therefore, dismissed the idea altogether at first. But over time, I have come to realize how simple and beautiful of a practice this can be.

Don't confuse mindfulness with meditation. Mindfulness simply requires you to be in the present. That's it! You may add meditation to your practice and grow your mindfulness overtime. Being mindful is simply disconnecting with anything that goes on inside of you and allowing yourself to exist with observation, curiosity, and gratitude. Meditation takes your practice further as you attempt to mindfully focus on an object, thought, or activity to achieve mental clarity and calm. There are many ways to meditate. I practice meditation through yoga, practicing various art forms, connecting with nature, and prayer. You can also try breath work or an activity that brings calmness. Adding spiritual elements to your practice can do wonders for your soul.

I invite you to slowly begin to challenge your mind to live in the present. Notice the moment, intentionally, to relieve yourself of the worries of past or future. What I love about this practice is that it allows us to live in ways that are less automatic. This means less time spent worrying, ruminating, and trying to control things we can't control, leaving those things in God's domain. It means we become less vulnerable to the fear-driven tendencies of our minds and open to our more sophisticated mental abilities like patience, compassion, acceptance, wonder, and reason.

Aside from my spiritual practices, I personally learned mindfulness through disconnecting with everything outside of the yoga studio and really bringing my focus into the hour-long classes. Leaving my phone outside the class, I imagine entering a new zone where no one can disturb me. I condition and prime myself for this mind, body, and breathwork activity. Through regular practice of hatha yoga, slowly, the effects trickled into my daily life. How I think and do things, how I pray, connect, and reflect. I learned to slow down and taste the beauty of things and move through life gracefully.

Conscious versus Unconscious

There is the intentional practice of conscious mindfulness that you struggle to achieve, which is normally taught in mindfulness classes and books. But there is also the unconscious mindfulness that just comes upon you spontaneously. You might be unaware, but you get such random impulses naturally, such as the times when you are in your own head, as usual, then you suddenly see/hear/smell something and are pulled out of your internal dialogue, right into the present (what a beautiful bird! Wow, look at that full moon! Such a fantastic view!) and you appreciate it fully, just for that moment. We just need to intentionally practice that more and more until it becomes our way of living.

Most people carry on their lives filled with mundane, repetitive routines without taking a moment to shift their minds into the beauty of the moment. For example, how many people look at the sky as soon as they exit their homes to go somewhere? Do they see the clouds? How about noticing the rattling trees and chirping birds?

To meet up with my coaching clients, I purposefully choose cafes, parks, or locations with views or something that would bring their awareness into the moment. I often ask my client to notice their surroundings a bit and practice pausing their racing thoughts and simply slow down and notice with a wider lens. Once, my client told me that everything in her life was a mess. I asked her, "Let's try to find something good in this moment?" She was so absorbed in her perceived reality of how bad her life was, that she couldn't notice the serene views outside the window, inviting her to reflect. By the end of our meeting, she had a new perspective!

I have made it a habit to take a deep long breath as I look up at the sky as I step outside. So many days through the month, I find the moon is visible in the sky in daylight, as if staring at me from up above, waiting to be noticed, reminding me in its own wisdom as if, to learn to be mysterious, humble, or hidden sometimes...allowing grace, knowing very well that it will shine bight with all its splendour in its own time.

Our unconscious autopilot mind is accustomed to masking the present moment with thoughts and worries about the past or future, attracting the same things repeatedly. If we consciously begin to see wonder, purpose, and blessing in our moment, we can dream and design our future with positive imagination.

It's amazing how masterful our ability is to have our body in one place and our mind somewhere else. It wanders with thoughts irrelevant to the present. To start, we need to shift our minds to our main task at hand. After regular practice it becomes a natural way of being.

On our automatic pilot mode, we are likely to get triggered easily. Our surroundings, thoughts, feelings, and perceptions in the mind, which we may only be dimly aware of, can trigger old habits of thinking patterns that are often difficult to regulate and have a negative impact on our attitudes. It can blur our vision and make things complicated for us. By becoming more consciously aware of our momentary thoughts, feelings, and physical sensations, we give ourselves the possibility of greater clarity, freedom, and choice. We allow ourselves to fully absorb our present experience and respond intentionally.

> *"Becoming awake involves seeing our confusion more clearly."*
> —Rumi

Most of our troubles are related to our view of everything. Now a days, there is too much external noise... information, opinions, standards etc. If we mindfully sit with ourselves, understanding our own path clearly, we can generate powerful responses from within. It slowly becomes a very cautious state of being. The more we choose to process everything that crosses our path mindfully, the more grounded we feel, the purposeful our responses, and the more enjoyable our experiences.

I'm reminded of Prophet Muhammad's (peace and blessings be upon him) example of giving special attention to ordinary people as he interacted with them ever so mindfully, giving all his courtesy and utmost concern to that person, while being the busiest man of his time. Each interaction would leave a high impact on the receiving end. The ordinary companion felt as though they were the most beloved and most cared for person in his eyes. It was his powerful presence that made them feel so special. Becoming totally present can have dramatic impact on ordinary interactions.

> *Wherever you are, be there totally.*
> —Eckhart Tolle

Mindfulness also means becoming aware of what we eat, wear, keep, and buy; anything we expose ourselves to in our surroundings; and how we keep our homes or workspaces. Check out the teachings of *Feng Shui*. It is an interesting, ancient Chinese way of arranging your surroundings in a positive way to support overall wellness. Or perhaps explore the concept of *minimalism* to reduce the noise and create a mindful space with fewer belongings that remind you of your values and purpose. When you design your surroundings mindfully, you facilitate desired results.

Finding Joy in Your Moments

When you learn to seize the moment, you experience the wonder and mystery that are always present in our world. I remember in the past when I would go out into nature, on road trips, or vacations, I wouldn't bring back too much more than the memorable events and pictures. As I have mindfully become more and more in sync with nature, I find myself lost in it every time we escape our city. I notice the clouds, the trees, the wildlife, and the mountains. I find myself communicating with nature. We really do live in a fairy tale, if we truly observe.

Once my awareness of my surroundings was awakened, my ability to direct my attention to the beauty and power of the present moment increased and so did the joy of the moment. Living in that state brought about the practice of immense glorification of the Almighty, awe, humility, and gratitude.

One may become aware that the present moment can also bring attention to the litter on the street, traffic jams, homeless in need, and make one feel upset. But once you become a problem solver or a growth seeker, you do anything in your ability to change a bad situation. Pick up the litter as you see it, imagine the trees greeting you, enjoy the scenery or beautiful skies during a traffic jam. Find reasons to be grateful for anything good. In doing so, you are living in the moment, feeling purposeful and happier as opposed to ignoring your surroundings due to your annoyances of the moment.

Instead of doing too many things mindlessly, we want to slow down a bit and do lesser things more mindfully. It is simply an intentional practice to notice thoughts, physical sensations, sights, sounds, smells . . . anything we might not normally notice. We practice focusing on details, which brings us towards reflecting on our blessings and deepening our spirituality. In the process, we begin to challenge ourselves creatively, which adds more joy to our present moment.

Practicing the Pause

Most of my mistakes in life were made when I rushed into things, didn't take my time, or felt compelled to say or do something when the right thing was simply to pause, think about it, give it time, or slow down. Wisdom kicks in when you give time and thought and be patient a little longer. I became aware that where I have passion and fierce action-taking attitude, I also need to balance with pausing, reflecting, and then accessing my inner wisdom. And what's exciting is that I'm exposed to an inner calm through delving deeper into my spirituality through practicing the pause.

There is a similar concept in mindfulness that is practiced in your body (according to my yoga teacher) called *practicing the pause*. This type of pause requires you to stop whatever you're doing to take deep breaths in and out. Focus on your lungs expanding and contracting. There's no rush to finish this process. It gets you out of your head and into your body. As such, it's a great process to help you reset any overwhelming emotions you may have been experiencing and get you into the moment.

Practicing the pause enhances our awareness of the moment. It is key to increasing our ability to choose how we respond. When we don't insert a pause between a stimulus and our response, we may wind up just reacting, which limits our choices and does potential damage, such as causing distress, guilt, shame, sadness, etc. Pausing allows us to own our responses. We can all work on this practice especially in current times where we are constantly distracted and interrupted and 'slowing down' seems challenging.

Non-Judgemental Awareness

Another aspect of mindfulness is living free of judgements. Judgements of oneself firstly, and then of others. As a highly self-critical and perfectionistic person in the past, I didn't quite understand this. How could I be better if I don't judge myself? Well, the key is to notice with care not criticism, so you can create room for growth. Seeing mistakes as just mistakes and not intentional wrongdoings or incapabilities. As you allow yourself such compassion, you expand yourself for others as well. You can see that this other person has potential and needs gentleness as opposed to criticism and hate.

So, if you cook a meal and it doesn't turn out as good, notice what went wrong and how you can change your recipe next time. Don't pass judgements, such as, I'm such a bad cook, or, What will so-and-so think? When stuck in traffic, notice the scene around you or perhaps enjoy your favourite audio book or podcast without the urge to say, I hate this daily drive, or I'm going to be late now. Just giving in to the fact that things will be out of our control and that we need to surrender and remain calm.

With my regular practice of yoga over the last decade, I learned that the practice revolves around you discovering, experimenting, focusing, relaxing, and challenging yourself without any competition or worry of judgements of others. How liberating! You are there to honour and work on yourself at your own pace. One person could be super advanced and flexible with their poses whereas another could be a beginner, barely able to fully bend forward. Everyone coexists in their respective practice working on their own goals. Basically, you focus your attention on noticing what exists in your present moment only and avoid any judgemental thoughts that cross your mind. You show up within the four corners of your yoga mat intentionally.

Judgement itself is a learned behavioural pattern. As humans, we are not naturally made to judge or feel judged. Have you seen how children will notice the smells, colours, and artsy details about their surroundings while adults busy themselves in passing judgements or remaining stuck in their worries? Children will also express freely and be more present. Perhaps we need more of that playful carefree imagination to begin living in the moment, kind of like children naturally know to do. Perhaps we are programed out of our beautiful natural inclination over time and the practice of becoming more mindful can help us renew our true essence. As we show up more neutrally, we can practice curiosity, which allows us to observe and gain clarity.

The Middle Path

Living mindfully requires for us to explore *lagom*, which is a moderate path in Swedish psyche. Not seeking too little or too much, rather just right balance in everything. I find this to be such a powerful concept, which is a vital teaching in Islam. The idea of choosing 'the middle path' means to know what is needed and what is not. Choosing the path straight in the middle, away from any extremes. Striking balance in all aspects of life. Not giving an area too much attention while ignoring other areas of life. Many people waste away their lives building hefty careers and accumulating wealth, while ignoring family connections, nourishing the mind, body, and soul. Knowing where you need moderation and awareness and learning how to sustain good balance in every aspect of your life is critical. Lagom allows for imperfection and freedom. Such mindful way of creating balance in one's life can promote overall contentment and an upgraded sense of self.

The call for moderation is embedded in all aspects of Muslim practice such as in prayer *i.e.* to not be too loud or too quiet. In expenditure, Allah commands to neither be extravagant nor miserly (Quran 25:67), or even in matters of consumption, the Quran teaches to "eat and drink and not exceed the limits." Similarly, living in this world with the awareness of the hereafter is significantly important in the Islamic tradition. In such a way, one develops a comprehensive balanced approach to living mindfully and purposefully.

How to Practice Mindfulness

A powerful way to practice mindfulness is to be fully present for each activity or conversation that you're involved with throughout the day. If something goes well, you take a moment, pause, and express gratitude in your heart. You can also be mindful by feeling grateful for things that could have gone wrong and didn't. And if you had a learning opportunity from a bad experience, notice it and be intentional about it. By doing so, you can build a habit of setting intentions, becoming more aware, and cultivating a growth mindset. Here are some ways to begin cultivating mindfulness in your life:

- Seeking connection with God through prayer and gratitude will enhance all practices of mindfulness.

- Slow down! Live your experience through focusing on your five senses to bring awareness to the moment.

- Create balance in your life. Don't get too fixated on one area in your life while ignoring others. A mindful life is a wholesome life.

- Meditate for five minutes in the morning and evening. Sit comfortably, close your eyes, and focus your attention on your breath. If you notice any tension in your body, breathe a sense of relaxation into that part of your body and exhale. If you become aware of any thoughts simply return to your breath.

- Practice a hobby or an art form that is meditative for you. Join a weekly session of an activity that helps you focus and indulge in the practice. Mandala meditative colouring, painting, knitting, gardening, or cooking classes are all great ideas for practicing mindfulness.

- Put the phone down! Engage fully in conversations. Listen to people and speak meaningfully. Make more eye contact. Be more intentional to enhance your momentary experiences.

Mindfulness grows your overall awareness, which allows you to be more intentional and in control of your life.

Reflect

1. How mindful are you currently in your day-to-day life? Rate from one to ten.
2. In what ways can you try to live more mindfully? Make a list.
3. What consistent action can you take to grow your practice?

*Be in this world as if you were a
stranger or a traveler along a path.*

—Prophet Muhammad
(peace be upon him)

Release Attachments

Non-attachment has been spoken about in many religions due to its importance in our attempts to ascend and get acquainted with our higher selves. We need to understand the vital importance of what it really means to live without letting the external things control and overpower our emotions and sense of happiness.

The most liberating concept that I want to introduce to you is releasing attachments to people, possessions, beliefs, customs, etc. You really will grow as much as you are open to challenging the status quo. If your goal is to live soulfully, following the crowds and trends aimlessly and chasing after attaining the current standards of materialistic accomplishments can be detrimental for your self-worth and purpose in life. You can't enrich your soul with peace and contentment if your inner vessel is filled with such attachments.

Your customary way of thinking and being, needs to be challenged so you can step into a better version of yourself. When we find it difficult to challenge our previously known ideologies, we remain stuck in a known bubble, which may be a reality we attach ourselves to. When we are willing to explore new possibilities and ideas, we are open to levelling up, attaining freedom and enlightenment.

Understanding Attachment

We are attached to many different things in life. Our attachments to people, things, and all the concepts we have about ourselves or life in general, shape our reality. Our attachments reflect what holds meaning in our lives and what we pursue. Our motivations and goals are based on these attachments, which can delude our pursuit for happiness and success.

Whether a person is religious or not, everyone has a God. Everyone worships something. To *worship* essentially means to have one's heart attached to something so much so that their life revolves around it. They strive towards attaining, preserving, taking care of, investing in, and pursuing more and more of this attachment.

As a Muslim, my God is Allah, whose worship and guidance is what my life revolves around. Seeking His pleasure and obedience is what fills my vessel. Even in the worldly things I pursue, I must follow His commands, making sure that I don't get attached to any objects. To worship, for me, entails all ways I can glorify God and remember Him through a soulful connection that is built as my heart attaches me to His awareness. This worship is manifested through my five timely prayers, fasting, giving charity, and supplications of remembering and showing gratitude towards Him. In each of these practices, I find myself detaching from my egoistic attachments and connecting back to my soul and remembering my bigger purpose.

Prayer requires for me to dedicate a few minutes in solitude and perform a set ritual mindfully. Giving charity cures my greed and allows me to purify my wealth as I detach myself from it. Practicing gratitude through various supplications makes me appreciate what I have gracefully. All these practices allow me to attach my heart to the Most High, Allah.

So, for a devout Muslim, it becomes clear that one doesn't get more attached to anything more than Almighty Allah/God to the extent of worshipping it. Yet, for most people, unintentionally, that object of worship is something from this life, which becomes their primary attachment.

People find such attachments in wealth, status, or fame, exhausting all their time and energies towards attaining more and more. Some may become obsessively attached to other people or even themselves. The Quran describes such people as "worshiping their own whims and desires." Other attachments can be to our belongings, our own image, our careers, or titles. Such false attachments deviate the heart and cause excessive obsessions, compulsions, or dissatisfactions in life.

Everything you have is on loan. Foolish is the one who gets attached to a loan.
—Yasmine Mugahed

What is non-Attachment?

It all goes back to the primary concept of developing a heightened sense of awareness, where a person simply understands the transient nature of material things and doesn't get too attached to them or the idea of ownership. Things may come and go, but your worth should not be attached to those things. You can love good things but cling on to nothing. If you were to lose an object of attachment, it doesn't cause devastation, rather you accept and flow with the changing seasons of life. Others' nice houses, fancy cars, or prestigious lives don't faze you when your heart is not attached to such things. Yes, admire and appreciate things; if you practice non-attachment, you will not feel jealousy or envy.

Same goes for people in your life. You can have great relationships without putting the strain on them to make you happy. You will truly honour the people in your life when you understand that humans are not infallible and will make mistakes and you will have to find ways to overlook them through practicing non-attachment. If you release the attachment to your predetermined expectations of people, you will genuinely love them without clinging on to them. Having a fall-out with a friend will mean just that, not much more.

Releasing attachments also means not getting too fixated on your thought systems, such as beliefs, customary trends, perceptions, ideologies, etc. Challenging things you believe about yourself or others, can be shifted to neutral and even positive. Many ideas are passed down to us through our generational programming. Some can be very beneficial for us and others, not so much. Detachment requires for us to remain open to new ideas and explore concepts that may change our lives for the better.

What we know of our self-beliefs, who we are, and what is possible for us is all real in the form of definitions that we make up for ourselves and are changeable. They all must remain open to be challenged. For example, you may accept any belief system without questioning it and struggle with owning it if you never questioned it, whether religious, personal, societal, or conceptual.

Non-Attachment is making peace with this idea that nothing in this life lasts forever. Living each moment as if it were your only moment the best possible way and not arguing against what the current moment presents, is the goal. To allow emotions to flow freely without getting too fixated on them. Taking joyfulness and sorrows as they come, with gratitude or patience, without getting attached to either. It is to fulfil your needs and not be tempted to make the *pursuit of more* your key objective.

Why Release Attachments?

Everywhere we look around us, there are traps that incite us to indulge in and seek worldliness. The growth of mass production, consumerism, designer brands, fueled by media advertisements have led to an insatiable appetite for more and more. This is a tragedy that one must become aware of and actively counter. If we focus on sustaining our *needs*, in a balanced way, we are conscious of what is beyond that. Many are wasting their lives chasing after all their *wants*.

There are no limits on our desire for wanting more, as the sole motivator for desire is pleasure. The more one acquires the more one desires. As you lose balance and follow your desires, you bear the consequences of your choices. Excessive greed leads to addiction, miserliness, and loss of inner peace. It can also impact relationships negatively. I once heard in a Friday sermon that the example of the seeker of one's desires is like the one who drinks salty water. The more you drink, the thirstier you become, and it never quenches your thirst!

Our attachments keep us busy with wanting more and more and keeps us away from the more meaningful yearnings that exist on a soulful level. In actuality, deep down inside, we all seek to disconnect from the worldly possessions and stressful expenditures so we can invest our energies into the deeper cravings of our souls, inviting freedom and joy. An *inner shift* is needed.

We are taught in religious texts to live each day as if it were your last. In Islam, we teach "Pray as if it's your last prayer." Why do we stress that? So, we can fully connect and detach from anything worldly as we show up the best way possible in that given act of worship. Many distinguished prophets and spiritual masters from the past lived simple lives with fewer belongings. They were content and successful. Their examples reflect the higher truth that material possessions are futile and fleeting.

Letting go of our attachments creates space for deeper awareness and curiosity. It puts the reality of our purpose in perspective for us and allows us to pursue it wholeheartedly. If you are always bogged down by the matters of attaining the next thing in life, you will never be able to strike the right balance to have enough time for your relationship with yourself, God, and loved ones.

Our stuff often accumulates stress and becomes our baggage and prevents us from seeing the real valuable things clearly. We get big houses and become married to them. We hoard our possessions and attach emotional value to them. The thought of letting go of things can be overwhelming because we become stuck in our belongings. When the truth is, our stuff is temporary and serves very limited purpose to our life's fulfilment. Much of our stuff is simply taking space in our lives without serving a real need.

We must declutter, recycle, give away, and choose a more minimalistic approach to living life. Minimalism can be practiced in a very different way from person to person, but it has genius magic in it. We feel happier and lighter when we own fewer possessions. It frees up our time, space, and energy to focus on more purposeful things and valuable experiences.

Attachment to Norms

In South Asian culture, women have this attachment to their gold jewelry that gets passed down to the next generation. As a tradition alone, it can be of some value. However, even in times of need, this gold is not touched. If you have the luxury to pass it down, sure, but when the need arises, it should be available to use. Our meaningless loyalties enslave us and make us stuck in old ways, depriving us of having peace of mind. Our wealth should work for us not against us. We seem to follow the traditions aimlessly just so we can show off and maintain an acceptable image.

Another classic example is how many cultural weddings take place after much money is saved in preparation. From serious spending and unnecessary waste to living up to other people's expectations, we end up increasing our stress levels more as opposed to enjoying the sacred union. What is all that expenditure and expectation based on? Our need to fulfill societal demands that have become trends we feel attached to.

Let's dare to go against the flow and challenge some of these trends that don't bring us much joy, but drain us. Why take on unwanted pressure? Rather, lets choose to have simpler, less extravagant, more genuine celebrations that reflect our values and bring us joy.

Most people tend to be set in their traditional ways. At times, you pick up ideologies from the way you were raised. You may have some *idea attachments* but be completely unaware of them. Simply start by asking yourself questions like, Where did this idea/thought come from? or, Do I really believe this to be true? or, What if I changed my perspective?

The more you incorporate *thought awareness* into your life, the more readily you'll see how irrelevant or changeable many thoughts are. Your thoughts only mean something when *you* assign them meaning. Train yourself to challenge your thoughts, trust your intuitions, and question things. Non-attachment to norms and trends allows us to be flexible and opens us to a more expansive perception of the world and everything around us.

Attachment to people

We get overly attached to people in our lives, be it our spouses, children, or close friends. So many people rely on codependency of sorts, which ultimately can bring about much distress. We end up falling into unhealthy patterns and insecurities because of our attachments to and expectations from other people. Being non-attached to people means to appreciate them for what they present to us in our relationship without the reliance on them to make us happy.

We are conditioned to believe that being in love and married to someone means holding them accountable for keeping us happy. They must fulfill our needs otherwise we feel unhappy or discontent. This attachment takes away responsibility from us and allows us to blame others for our unhappiness. You are two whole individuals in a relationship, not two halves that must complete each other, as you may have been convinced to believe. A healthy relationship requires detaching from such ideologies and investing to grow together.

Let's notice our manipulative attachments to the concept of love for our children. Most of the times, having their love and giving them love depends on whether they fulfill our dreams and ideals about how they need to be under our supervision regardless of their unique personalities, aspirations, needs, or wants. Parents get obsessed with their expectations of how the children must live.

Have you seen how many parents force their vision of success onto their children? Sometimes they literally choose and impose professions on them and obsessively control their lives based on their own desires. So many parents do this unconsciously because they are simply enslaved to their attachments to societal pressures and want to prove something to others. And as the children grow older and go on to live their own lives, there are more expectations that take away much peace of mind. Many of you have experienced this pressure growing up and you may be doing this to your own children as well.

Many parents only offer conditional love to their children based on their attachment to certain expectations. Are we allowing them to blossom in their best ways or are we trying to get them to fulfill our ideas of what they *should* do in life because of who *we* are? Many parents don't understand this, but if we become open to letting go of the idea of controlling and imposing ourselves upon children, we free ourselves and allow more growth and possibility for our children in their lives as well as in our relationships.

We can teach, love, and support them but without manipulation. We can heal generational patterns by allowing more open-minded parenting that is detached from old concepts and pressures. We can love anyone in our lives without getting too attached to them in obsessive controlling ways.

Sadly, we are ignorantly attached to our conditioned twisted concepts, which lead to egoistic distortions, such as emotional manipulating, holding grudges, becoming insecure, self-sabotaging, and game playing. How can we thrive as spouses, parents, or friends when our hearts are filled with all that junk? We must challenge our ideologies and break through our limiting patterns that keep us stressed and unhappy inside.

Don't we also get too attached to gurus, teachers, leaders, celebrities, or other attractive personalities? Yes, we may find inspiration through admirable personalities, but we should look beyond the illusions they create. If we blindly attach ourselves, we are at risk of idolizing them which can be misleading for our inner purpose. It detaches us from ourselves and God. When we put others on a pedestal, we forget they are also humans and will disappoint us if they don't measure up to our idealized standards in some way. Detachment requires for us to not be enamored with whoever guides us and stay focused on the message they present.

How to Release Attachments

Non-attachment is a journey that we slowly embrace as we begin to detach ourselves from our egoistic tendencies and connect to our soulful beings. Let me share some useful ways to release attachments:

- Live a simple life. Try to cut down on unnecessary exposure to materialism, following trends, comparisons, reliance on others, or media.
- Find joy in life's simple pleasures. Don't trivialize the beauty around you and the blessings you can be grateful for.
- Destress yourself by eliminating negative influence. Declutter your life by giving away/selling stuff you don't need or by cancelling subscriptions to services you don't use. Detox your life from false illusions of happiness.

- Attach yourself to a higher purpose. Pursue activities that help connect you with yourself, your loved ones, nature, and promote holistic well-being. Give charity and help others.

- Invite gratitude through expanding what you have. Abundance is not in accumulation of things, rather an acquired inner feeling.

- Think outside the box. Eliminate extreme thought patterns and invite new enlightening perspectives.

- Grow personal discipline by remaining firm on your habits and routines. This will ground you and develop personal control and resilience.

> *Detachment is not that you should own nothing, but that nothing should own you.*
> —Ali Ibn Abi Talib

Furthermore, use this recognition to fuel your pursuit to find that which is eternal. For me, it always comes back to attaching myself to Allah (God) and exploring ways to fill my soul through that connection.

Reflect

1. Notice and journal about how much of your day is spent obsessing about a physical thing or possession of the past, present, or future. In what ways can you practice detachment?

2. Bring awareness towards your expectations of other people in your life and see whether you can challenge or let go of them.

3. What are some of your limiting *self-beliefs* that you hold as truths in your mind? Question them. Are they true? How can you shift them?

4. How can you simplify your life?

*When you are grateful,
fear disappears and
abundance appears.*

—Tony Robbins

Grow Your Gratitude

Do you want more from life? More happiness? Better health? Successful relationships? Spirituality? Confidence? Productivity? Well, here's the secret, practice gratitude! I am passionate about inspiring those I coach to cultivate an *attitude of gratitude* in their lives. The fruits of this practice can take care of many other problems you might face.

Most people are focused on what's next in life. They are either stuck in the past or worried about the future. There is this emptiness, a gap that needs to be filled. The whole mindset of "If I get this, then I'll be happy/ good enough/ successful, etc." takes away our ability to sit where we are in gratitude. It robs us of our peace of mind and keeps us agitated. We are not able to truly taste the sweetness of feeling blessed and sink into the feeling of being content. The true essence of tasting *abundance,* in our current state with humility, is a tact one must explore, learn, and in due time, master, to be happy.

This is also why in nearly all religions; prayers of gratitude exist in some form. In Islam, where I derive most of my life wisdoms from, there is great emphasis on showing gratitude towards Allah/God and humanity through various acts of worship and prayers.

What Is Gratitude?

We have all been thankful in life. Where thankfulness is merely expressed in words, *gratitude* is far deeper. It is a state of being and a way of doing. Gratitude is a beautiful feeling and a humble concept. It is building the habit of not only believing that you are blessed, but also expressing it through your words and actions. A grateful soul looks for evidence of little wonders in life, incomparable to anyone else's.

Train yourself to feel grateful for what's good in your ordinary lifestyle, *here and now*. If you are not happy with what you have right now, chances of becoming happier when you have more are slim. Very often, people notice what they don't have in their lives. They complain about how their lives aren't good enough compared to others. Maybe their looks are not up to the customary standards. Perhaps they feel unfortunate in how things turned out for them compared to others.

We need to make a conscious effort to recognize what we have, irrespective of what others have, filtering out the societal conditioning of what we *should* have. When you decide to notice all that you already have, you stop taking anything for granted and begin to cherish it all. Focusing on your own goals and ambitions becomes easier and more enjoyable.

One must practice such an attitude deliberately until it becomes an inbuilt habit. In return, you will begin to feel a sense of appreciation as you enjoy life's small pleasures. Try to acknowledge little things that normally go unnoticed by many and take the time to express your appreciation.

Benefits of Practicing Gratitude

If you take a holistic approach to understanding overall well-being, you'll discover that people who regularly practice gratitude experience more positive emotions, feel content, sleep better, express more compassion, and have stronger immune systems. Having an attitude of gratitude saves you from feelings of sadness and jealousy. It allows you to invite abundance into your life.

Practicing gratitude helps us increase our capacity for receiving. So many of us struggle with receiving compliments and owning our successes. I've noticed especially that women tend to deflect compliments and praise due to the feelings of unworthiness. The more gratitude we learn to express, the more comes our way and we in return, get to receive it wholeheartedly. One of my favourite mindset mantras is: *ask, believe, receive!* It is the concept of *law of attraction*. So, the more gratitude you practice, the more you will receive.

I want to bring your attention to yet another interesting perspective on gratitude. What is the opposite of gratitude? Well, ingratitude, of course! But there's more… If you go a little deeper and practice living with gratitude, you'll discover all these other opposites such as:

- *Fear*. Because being thankful for everything can lead us to welcome anything even the things that scare us. We learn to be accepting of challenges with a more positive outlook when we practice gratitude.

- *Loneliness*. Because feeling grateful connects us with God and those around us, which makes us more charismatic without even trying. With the abundance we experience, we feel satisfied. Spending time alone doesn't sadden us.

- *Anxiety*. Because choosing to think on the tremendous blessings in life, instead of what challenges life brings, wards off our worries. With such an attitude, we also embrace our challenges with a smile.

- *Anger*. Because while anger is hating the way things are, gratitude is loving what is. With the practice of gratitude, we overcome the displeasure with our lives and show gentleness in our affairs.

Adopting an overall attitude of gratitude through building necessary habits and practices can have an enormous amount of impact on personal growth. Many of our emotional problems such as envy, anger, stress, and anxiety can be cured by simply living a bit more consciously and being aware of all the life's blessings. Cultivate the practice of expressing your gratitude towards your Creator, people, and, most of all, yourself to feel fulfilled in life.

Ways to Practice Gratitude

One way to truly appreciate what we already have is by occasionally reflecting on the possibility of losing the people and possessions in our lives. Truly anything we currently have is a gift to us, even if we worked for it, because even the ability to work for the things we enjoy is not given to everyone. Our destined life, health, our sanity, people around us, things, and many other pleasant happenings are gifts that we must recognize and show gratitude for. Many others, simply by destiny, don't have what we do. By contemplating the loss of what we love, including our lives, can really ground us in gratitude. This practice is also called *negative visualization,* which is a powerful technique and an antidote to grow gratitude and boost our capacity for inviting joy.

Try keeping a gratitude journal. Gratitude journaling works because it gradually changes the way we perceive situations by adjusting our focus. While you might always be thankful for your wonderful family, just writing "I'm grateful for my family" doesn't keep your creative mind observant for new grateful moments. Get more specific by writing, "Today I'm grateful that my girls cleaned the kitchen for me" or "I got to enjoy time out in nature and get my mind off of stressful things." Being mindful of those detailed observations can be quite eye opening.

Be sure to extend yourself beyond the obvious things and look a little deeper. Opening your mind to more of the world around you can deeply enhance your gratitude practice. Try noticing new things each day. At the end of the day, write down a few things big or small that you can be grateful for. Go back to read your journal, it will melt your heart and fill it with joy and comfort. This activity can be practiced in other creative ways as well. If you don't enjoy writing in a journal, you can create an online or voice recorded journal or have a family gratitude conversation regularly.

The prophet Muhammad (peace be upon him) said:

"Look at those below you but not those above you because you will become ungrateful" (*Sahih Muslim,* 7070).

Now this is in context of blessings and worldly possessions. One must look to those above them for inspiration and growth. To attain humility and gratitude however, one needs to feel abundant in their current state. It takes some practice to frame your mind with such grateful thoughts, but once practiced long enough, you are wired to think like that.

Gratitude should not be reserved for life events such as getting a job, the people we love, or things we own. Just noticing all the situations that could have been uncomfortable, such as before you shower, you can be grateful for having warm water. Before you sleep, you can be thankful for not having to sleep on the floor in some refugee camp as you enjoy the comfort of your cozy warm bed in a safe home. Going to bed with that mindset can never be stressful, sad, or depressing no matter what you went through that day.

That awareness of having enough and being happy with our situations can put our hearts in tremendous amount of peace and serenity.

What separates privilege from entitlement is gratitude.
—Brené Brown, *The Gifts of Imperfection*

You can exercise gratitude privately and express it with others. Our relationships with others are crucial for our happiness. So, we must think of other people as we develop our gratitude practice. You can begin to build a habit of showing gratitude to people for their contributions and efforts. Write thank you notes to family or friends. Convey your heartfelt gratitude through words, gestures, and conduct. Make those around you feel appreciated and acknowledged. Think of creative ideas to surprise others with compliments and positive feedback. It will be fulfilling for you, and they will feel recognized as well.

There is a kind of gratitude one expresses while receiving and yet there's a higher level of this practice; the kind we feel when we give. When you share some of what you have, the beautiful feeling you get inside is immense! It could be knowledge, wealth, time, or even emotional support. Giving simply happens easily and more joyfully when you begin to feel grateful and blessed. Your cup is so full that pouring from it becomes easier, which truly fills your soul. Try a few of these ways to expand your practice of gratitude:

- Stop complaining about little things. Be mindful of using phrases that bring about thankfulness and avoid using complaining language.

- Journal or share what you're grateful for every day.

- Switch your negative thought with a positive one until it become your habitual way of thinking.
- Reflect on the temporary nature of everything good or bad. As you are patient with your challenges, you'll feel more grateful for your blessings.
- Smile more often.

Reflect

1. Catch yourself being ungrateful or complaining about something. Exchange that thought or feeling with a grateful one and write it down.

2. Start your morning with a minute-long ritual of counting your blessings. Anything at all that you are grateful for, think of it and express it. Write in a journal or share with someone close to you.

3. Think of ways to express gratitude towards others and commit to an action step you will take this week.

The more awake one is to the material world, the more one is asleep to spirit.

—Rumi

Cultivate Spirituality

While in different cultures, *spirituality* can mean different things to different people, according to my Islamic understanding, it is clearly connecting everything back to God and the purpose of this life. In Islam, spirituality means to have deep awareness of the origin of the universe, worshiping and submitting to God, growing humility, and mindful living, which all manifest through one's thoughts and actions.

In this way, an individual's relationship with Allah (God) is the focal point of Islamic spirituality. And the beauty of it all is that one can develop a more profound connection at any time. There is always a higher place to be with one's connection to God, oneself, and the deeper meaning of life. If you desire to live a fulfilled, grounded, righteous, and awakened life alongside growing your mind, I urge you to bring your focus towards cultivating spirituality.

Cultivating spirituality is important because it gives a more holistic picture to the overall human experience. One can't be focused on building a certain area in life while ignoring others. We all have a mind, body, and soul, which equally demand our attention. Human souls are created with true inner knowing. People are mostly shy to admit that they have a yearning to connect everything deeply to the ultimate source. They are scared to admit their intrinsic spiritual inclinations or even bring up the topic of spirituality in a society that is secular and disconnected with God or a bigger purpose that is beyond their limited existence on earth.

One should not make worldly pleasures the primary goal of this life. This is why we must contemplate death often. Through constant reminders of the undeniable truth of death, we can reduce our desire for such pleasures and enhance our overall awareness of this life and what comes after it.

Frequently remember the destroyer of pleasures (death).

—Prophet Muhammad (peace be on him)

Today, even with technological and scientific advancements, we are still unable to overcome our anxieties related to death. It baffles my mind to think that no one on this earth questions the reality of death, yet most live in this world as if it will last forever. We plan for it and exhaust all our time and efforts in building a good life. As if this was the ultimate destination. But we all know life ends, without announcing when.

No matter how much progress we make visibly as humankind, the need of feeding our soul remains vital. Even though more and more people are disconnected from and unaware of their spiritual needs, now, more than ever, the indulgence of the material life can be distracting and deceptive. This causes humans to forget the purpose of their lives. According to Islamic spirituality, the body perishes but the spirit remains forever. Therefore, tending to the spirit is vital.

Becoming spiritual requires conscious *inner shifting,* which builds our 'reflective muscle.' Going a little deeper within oneself entails questioning, exploring, connecting, praying, and being vulnerable. This requires time and energy and slowing down, which then brings clarity and purpose in many other areas. We are generally hesitant to do all that deep work in the western society, where people think of spirituality as something to merely distract themselves with from reality. I invite you to try exploring the exact opposite: a way of enrichment of the soul through rejoicing a deep meaningful connection.

What Is Spiritual Living?

Being spiritual has everything to do with your state of consciousness.

—Eckhart Tolle

Living a spiritual life can be a powerful experience. When you seek to understand things on a deeper level, you uncover signs and mysterious messages from above. Spirituality is not only an enhanced soulful connection to God; it is a deeper connection with oneself and the nature around us also. The more we understand the universe, the more we understand the Maker and the bigger hidden messages begin to reveal themselves. When we allow an overall deeper connection, we overlook the nuances that often take over our lives and stay focused on the bigger picture. We heal better and grow better. We seek better and understand better.

We can explore spirituality through different ways, alongside reflecting on religious scripture and teachings. After all, the ultimate goal of religion is to expand our consciousness and spirituality, however, many view it merely as a set of strict beliefs and guidelines or rituals. When you become more cognizant, you can't follow anything blindly. Everything becomes intentional and clear, which makes your practice more powerful.

For me, practicing Islam is also about refinement of the soul, aside from just fulfilling its commandments and external practices. My soul must surrender to an unseen external source in one way or another. In my view, understanding and recognizing the presence of a higher power in all our matters is spiritual growth. It allows me to surrender to where the divine plan overlaps and exceeds my personal capacity. My spirituality helps me with shifting inwards, developing humility, making better choices, and treating others in ways that make me feel aligned with my greater goal. It allows me to truly know where I can expand and grow and what not to resist. It keeps me rooted in my existence in relation to my purpose, my legacy, and my end. It allows me to develop a devout connection with the One who is above all.

When I experience a level of spirituality, with extensive admiration, I notice the sunsets, the moon's beauty, the colours of the sky, the glorious mountains, the trees, and all nature's treasures. Our existence is filled with opportunities to ponder on the ways of the universe. Stopping to smell the flowers and enjoying the colours of nature as we glorify the Creator, knowing that He didn't create anything in vain. I want to appreciate and examine everything with curiosity.

The unexamined life is not worth living.
—Socrates

Deriving deep messages from the universe can be very meaningful and comforting. For example, how the barren lands become green again, how spring follows winter, how the sun shows up after the night, systematically, in perfect, harmonious order. How the moon gracefully goes through its many phases. How the children from a poor village seem to be more content and joyful in contrast to those who seem to have all the luxuries of the worldly life. Or how incredibly my body functions, each organ delivers in most sophisticated ways. The more I look deeply, the more I wonder and develop profound understanding. It helps me understand how miraculous all creation is, including myself, and just how much potential is possible for greatness. The more in awe I look at the evidence in all systems of life around me, the more courage as well as humility fills my soul.

What if, we truly decided to live with the awareness that, it was our souls that possessed our bodies rather than our bodies that possessed our souls? Our simple everyday experience can turn into a more meaningful one if lead with our souls. It is through tapping into our spirituality that we understand the cravings of our souls as we access our intuitions more powerfully. The need to connect, understand, and think bigger than our small lives is all part of our intrinsic soul-driven nature.

A human requires a good balance of physical, mental, emotional, and spiritual well-being. Everything that I share in this book can essentially be practiced and adopted more efficiently with enhanced spirituality.

Benefits of Spiritual Growth

When you grow your spiritually, you can discover some of these benefits:

- You bring awareness and mindfulness to your existence, which can significantly change the meanings of your life experiences.
- Your solitude becomes sacred to you. You're able to pause, reflect, pray, meditate, and find stillness, which enlightens and enriches your life.
- You lead with gratitude and humility.

- You can practice detachment and find fulfilment in simple things.

- You learn to rely on a higher power and a divine plan. You can accept human limitations and receive various challenges gracefully and find new positive meanings within setbacks.

- You can easily purify your soul by overcoming resentment, anger, jealousy, anxiety, and unresolved grief through going deeper within and finding your soulful connection with the Almighty.

How to Grow Spirituality

There are numerous ways to grow your spirituality. You can create spiritual opportunities through allowing yourself to pause and contemplate on life, purpose, death, systems in nature, and creatures of all kinds. Here are some ideas for you to try for a spiritual boost, some of which will be a repetition of some sort from a previously shared chapter:

- Talk to God. Build a solid connection with Him through prayer and supplication. Share your inner longings with Him. Express gratitude for little blessings and cherished moments.

- Connect with nature. Notice the perfection in the creation all around us. Take nature walks as you deep breath the fresh air. Observe the sounds of flowing water and the chirping birds. As you feel in sync with everything around you, it will inevitably connect you to your Creator.

- Learn to rejoice your small moments of solitude by being mindfully present in the *now*. Distance yourself from the worries of the past or future and connect with momentary experiences. Find ways to surrender and feel more grounded.

- Let go of the ego and its demands, perhaps by slowing down, questioning and reflecting on your choices to arrive at a deeper meaning of things in your life.

- Ebb and flow, through pain and through pleasure, without getting too attached to your expectations. Allow change and search for a deeper meaning in everything.
- Help others in need. Volunteer. Performing acts of kindness and giving in charity can be phenomenal for spiritual growth.
- Connect with spiritual people and consume content that inspires you to grow your practice.
- Remember death often. It is a reality no one rejects, yet everyone lives as if they don't believe in it.

It's living through your soul that you find spirituality. It's thinking about your temporary life and what follows it. Reflecting on your preconceived notions and how you view life and its complexities in the grand scheme of things. Exploring your true self and the beauty in true nature of all creation. Allowing human experience to manifest through your way of living intuitively as it was intended by the Creator by design, with wonder, gratification, and purpose.

As you grow your spirituality, you meet your version of a *higher self*. You may have your lows at times, but you may also be pleasantly surprised at how transcendent you find yourself to be. Spiritual growth can foster unimaginable potential for shifting within to transform your life exponentially.

Reflect

1. How do you rate your current level of spirituality between one and ten?
2. How can boosting your spirituality change your life?
3. List a few small ways you intend to grow your spirituality.

References

Brown, Brené. 2015. *Daring Greatly.* Penguin Publishing Group.

—. 2010. *Gifts of Imperfection.* Simon & Schuster.

—. 2017. *Rising Strong.* Random House Publishing Group.

Covey, Stephen R. 2020. *The 7 Habits of Highly Effective People: Powerful Lessons in Personal Change.* UK Ltd: Simon & Schuster.

Dweck, Carol S. 2007. *Mindset: The new Psychology of Success.* New York: Ballantine Books.

Gilbert, Elizabeth. 2016. *Big Magic: Creative Living Beyond Fear.* NewYork: Penguin Publishing Group.

Hardy, Darren. 2012. *The Compound Effect.* USA: Vanguard Press .

Logue, Bernadette. 2014. *Unleash your Life.* Pinch Me Publishing.

Robbins, Tony. 1991. *Awaken the Giant Within.* Simon & Schuster.

—. n.d. *Tony Robbins.* Accessed 2021.

https://www.tonyrobbins.com/stories/unleash-the-power/discover-your-peak-state/.

Tolle, Eckhart. 1999. *The Power of Now: A guide to Spiritual Enlightenment.* New World Library.

Wooden, John. n.d. Accessed 2022.

https://www.thewoodeneffect.com.

Relevant Quotes

"No one will reap except what they sow."
   —Quran 6:164

"Take advantage of five before five: your youth before your old age, your health before your sickness, your wealth before your poverty, your free time before your busyness, and your life before your death."
   —Prophet Muhammad (pbuh)

"Those who look for seashells will find seashells; those who open them will find pearls."
   —Al-Ghazali

"What really counts are good endings, not flawed beginnings."
   —Ibn Taymiyyah

"Happiness is attained by three things: being patient when tested, being thankful when receiving a blessing, and being repentant upon sinning."
   —Ibn Qayyim Al-Jawziyya

"Richness does not exist outwardly. Verily, true richness is the richness of the soul."
   —Prophet Muhammad (pbuh)

"Collect as precious pearls the words of the wise and virtuous."
   —Abd El-Kader

"You have to grow from the inside out. None can teach you; none can make you spiritual. There is no other teacher but your own soul."
   —Swami Vivekananda.

"Look deep into nature, and then you will understand everything better."
  —Albert Einstein.

"Absorb what is useful. Discard what is not. Add what is uniquely your own."
  —Bruce Lee

"What lies behind us, and what lies before us, are tiny matters compared to what lies within us."
  —Ralph Waldo Emerson

"The more and more each is impelled by that which is intuitive, or the relying upon the soul force within, the greater, the farther, the deeper, the broader, the more constructive may be the result."
  —Edgar Cayce.

"If we want to succeed, we need to recover our grandparents' work ethic."
  — Darren Hardy

"People change when they ... Hurt enough that they have to, Learn enough that they want to, and Receive enough that they are able to."
  —John C. Maxwell

"When you replace 'why is this happening to me?' to 'what is this trying to teach me?' everything shifts."
  — Unknown

"Everyone is affected by three kinds of influences: input (what you feed your mind), associations (the people with whom you spend time), and environment (your surroundings)."
  — Darren Hardy

"The best victory is to conquer self."
  —Plato

"Smooth seas do not make skillful sailors."
  —African Proverb

"Success is a journey, not a destination. It requires constant effort, vigilance and re-evaluation."
—Mark Twain

"The turning point in your life is when you decide that your life is your own. No apologies or excuses. No one to expect from, rely on, or blame. You are responsible for the quality of your life's experience. That's where magic begins."
—Seema Khan

"A valuable book I can recommend for many of my patients struggling emotionally or mentally with life's challenges. The impact of which can be detrimental to one's health. Seema provides helpful insight that can combat this and improve overall well-being."
—Dr. Naila Sherwani

About the Author

Seema is a Canadian born Pakistani Muslim woman who wears many hats. She's a professional artist, educator, motivational speaker, author, and a certified holistic life coach. Seema has been married for over 20 years and is a mom to four amazing, homeschooled children. Her purpose, spirituality, personal well-being, and family are her top priorities in life. She loves to indulge in mindful practices such as yoga, connecting with nature, meditative art, nurturing her plants, and reflective writing. Seema is trained in various coaching fields and uses different modalities and tools such as NLP, IFS, Art Therapy, CBT, and Positive Psychology in her practice. She enjoys learning and intends to remain a student of knowledge to grow her skillset and deliver exceptional support to empower others. She also dedicates some time to mentoring moms by engaging in non-profit work.

As a holistic life coach, Seema works with women to overcome their mental and emotional challenges, empowering them to lead with  awareness, confidence, and purpose. Helping women build a strong sense of self, happier relationships, and parenting consciously, are most fulfilling in her work. Seema is enthusiastic about intentional, soulful living and cultivating self-mastery, which she believes impact all aspects of personal life. Her strong intuition and enhanced emotional intelligence are her most valuable gifts that she uses in her sessions. Seema believes that everyone has the potential to shift and bring about massive positive transformation in life.

Seema's work *The Inner Shift* is inspired by her personal journey, valuable Islamic teachings, her passion for helping others, vast research, and learnings through working directly with many happy clients.

Connect with Seema:

www.sisterinfocus.com

seema@sisterinfocus.com

seema.holisticlifecoach

Printed in Canada